Praise for *Heaven's Just a Prayer Away*

"*Heaven's Just a Prayer Away* is a sweet, heartfelt book with author Diony George's personal experiences intermixed with compelling stories about how prayer can shape our lives. I found myself either smiling or teary-eyed as I immersed myself in the stories, reminded that prayer is healing and sanctifying, prayer can bring inspiration, prayer can ease burdens, and prayer lets us feel the love of God for ourselves and those around us.

—**Heather B. Moore,** author of *Christ's Gifts to Women*

"In *Heaven's Just a Prayer Away*, Diony provides a comprehensive discussion on prayer through inspiring stories, basic principles, and heartfelt testimony. Her personal approach makes answers to prayer and divine blessings seem more within reach."

—**John McConkie,** stake president

HEAVEN'S
just a PRAYER *away*

HEAVEN'S *just a* PRAYER *away*

DIONY GEORGE

CFI
An Imprint of Cedar Fort, Inc.
Springville, Utah

ISBN 13: 978-1-4621-1189-3

Published by CFI, an imprint of Cedar Fort, Inc., 2373 W. 700 S., Springville, UT 84663
Distributed by Cedar Fort, Inc., www.cedarfort.com

Library of Congress Cataloging-in-Publication Data on file

Cover design by Erica Dixon, back cover by Shawnda T. Craig
Cover design © 2013 Lyle Mortimer
Edited and typeset by Emily S. Chambers

Printed in the United States of America

10 9 8 7 6 5 4 3 2 1

Printed on acid-free paper

Other books by Diony George

Torn Apart
Imperfectly Beautiful
A Sisterhood of Strength

Dedicated to my five sons, over whom I've prayed many prayers.

Contents

Nothing is too small or unimportant to pray about.

Chapter 1

His Gift to Us

"He will direct thee for good." —Alma 37:37

The pounding of my five-year-old heart slowed as I shut the front door and clicked the dead bolt in place. I wiped the remaining trail of fallen tears off my cheeks and ran to find my mom. Minutes earlier I'd gotten off the school bus at the usual stop, my friend and fellow classmate beside me—laughing together over something. We started down the hill. At the corner she saw her mom waiting in their car. She smiled and hurried over to her after telling me a quick good-bye. I watched her get in, feeling an instant twinge of loneliness at the sudden loss of company. I turned away, anxious to hurry home.

A man in a white car drove past me on the road. The flash of red taillights filled me with alarm as I watched him pull off to the shoulder in front of me. A surge of adrenaline kicked in. It had been less than two weeks since I'd started kindergarten, and the warning talk about "stranger danger" I'd gotten from my parents was fresh in my mind. Certain I was about to be kidnapped or worse, I raced back up the hill, crying and praying I could catch my friend.

I rounded the corner, seeing her car moving away, and started to yell. Her mom noticed me in the rearview mirror and stopped. When

I reached the driver's side, I was out of breath and terrified—the white car had followed me.

My friend's mom opened her door and asked me what was wrong. As I shakily explained, the man gunned his engine and swerved around us, leaving a cloud of dust. She offered to take me home. On the way she told me he had probably just missed his turn.

Maybe—but I *knew* Heavenly Father had heard my prayer.

Modern-day prophets have taught that before any of us came to earth, we lived in heavenly realms. We walked with our Heavenly Father. We knew Him. We heard His voice. We loved Him.

While we are here, we no longer have that same privilege and we must exercise our faith. But we need His guidance more than ever before. He gave us a gift—prayer—through which we can still turn to him for anything at anytime and anyplace. He is always listening and ready to help. He wants to hear from us, and prayer makes it easy.

Our prayers are most effective when we are trying to follow the commandments and stay close to the Spirit. When we are humble and our heart is in the right place, prayer can give us guidance and bring us peace.

It doesn't matter if our words aren't eloquent or if we struggle to express our feelings, we are talking with our Father, and His love for us is perfect. If we listen, we can recognize He is near. Making a wrong choice or a bad decision can make us feel as if He is unapproachable; in reality, that is when we need to turn to Him the most.

> No earthly authority can separate us from direct access to our Creator. There can never be a mechanical or electronic failure when we pray. There is no limit on the number of times or how long we can pray each day. There is no quota of how many needs we wish to pray for in each prayer. We do not need to go through secretaries or make an appointment to reach the throne of grace.
>
> Each of us has problems that we cannot solve and weaknesses that we cannot conquer without reaching out through prayer to a higher source of strength. That source is the God of heaven to whom we pray in the name of Jesus Christ.[1]

One of the earliest records of prayer was recorded by Moses, "And Adam and Eve, his wife called upon the name of the Lord, and they heard the voice of the Lord from the way toward the Garden of Eden, speaking unto them, and they saw him not;" (Moses 5:4).

In Alma, we're counseled to pray continually:

> Yea, and cry unto God for all thy support; yea, let all thy doings be unto the Lord, and whithersoever thou goest let it be in the Lord; yea, let all thy thoughts be directed unto the Lord; yea, let the affections of thy heart be placed upon the Lord forever.
>
> Counsel with the Lord in all thy doings, and he will direct thee for good; yea, when thou liest down at night lie down unto the Lord, that he may watch over you in your sleep; and when thou risest in the morning let thy heart be full of thanks unto God; and if ye do these things, ye shall be lifted up at the last day. (Alma 37:36–37)

I'm unable to remember a time from my childhood to the present when I haven't had the unquestionable knowledge that God hears my prayers. Prayer is as much a part of my life as breathing. I pray vocally but most often in my mind. Sometimes I wonder if the angels laugh, shake their heads, and say, "It's her again, Lord."

I know without a doubt praying changes things.

"Prayer is a heavenly gift designed to help us achieve spiritual lift. . . . Daily simple, sincere, and mighty prayers lift our lives to a higher spiritual altitude. . . . Prayer helps us transcend the stormy times. It gives us a glimpse of that blue sky we cannot see from our earthly vantage point, and it reveals to us another vista—a glorious spiritual horizon filled with hope and the assurance of the bright blessings the Lord has promised to those who love and follow him."[2]

A little orphan boy needed an operation for appendicitis. As he lay on the operating table, he looked at the faces of the surgeons and nurses around him. He addressed the surgeon in charge, "Doctor, before you begin to operate, will you pray for me?"

The surgeon's eyebrows raised above his surgical mask. "Why, I can't pray for you."

The boy turned to each person on the operating team and asked them one at a time, "Will you pray for me?"

Each of them declined.

"If you won't pray for me, won't you please wait while I pray for myself?" The little fellow got up on the operating table on his knees, folded his hands, and bravely prayed out loud.

"Heavenly Father, I am only a little orphan boy but I am awful sick, and these doctors are going to operate. Will you please help them that they will do it right? And now, Heavenly Father, if you make me well, I will be a good boy. Thank you for making me well."

He turned over and lay down again on his back. The room was filled with a hushed silence. Each doctor and nurse had tears in their eyes. The little boy softly said, "Now I am ready."

A few days later a man went into the office of the chief surgeon and asked to hear the details of the operation he had performed on that little boy.

The surgeon said, "That was the most remarkable experience of my whole life. I have operated on hundreds of men, women, and children, and I have known some of them to pray, but never until I stood in the presence of that little boy, have I heard anyone talk to their Heavenly Father face to face."

God is no respecter of persons, regardless of age, background, the color of our skin, or circumstances. When we are ready to turn to Him, He is ready to come to us. He will meet us wherever we are at, even if our life is full of sin and we feel unworthy. Even the devil knows this.

A wise man once declared, "Satan trembles, when he sees the weakest Saint upon his knees."[3]

God stands willing and waiting to encircle us in His unconditional love.

"But they that wait upon the Lord shall renew their strength; they shall mount up with wings as eagles; they shall run, and not be weary; and they shall walk, and not faint" (Isaiah 40:31).

NOTES

1 James E. Faust, "The Lifeline of Prayer," *Ensign*, May 2002.

2 Dieter F. Uchtdorf, "Prayer and the Blue Horizon," *Ensign*, June 2009.

3 William Cowper, *Poems Volume II*, Printed by E. Lincoln, for Manning & Loring, Boston, 1802, 31.

Chapter 2

Draw Near unto Him

"Seek me diligently and ye shall find me."
—Doctrine and Covenants 88:63

When I start the morning on my knees with sincere prayer, I feel a difference all day long knowing that nothing will happen that the Lord and I can't handle together. When I don't, the distractions of the world crowd in fast and furious, and it's hard to hear the quiet warnings and promptings of the Holy Ghost.

"Draw near unto me and I will draw near unto you; seek me diligently and ye shall find me; ask, and ye shall receive; knock, and it shall be opened unto you"(Doctrine and Covenants 88:63).

I remember hearing the following poem as a youth during a talk given in sacrament meeting. It has stuck with me ever since:

I got up early one morning and rushed right into the day.
I had so much to accomplish, I didn't have time to pray.
Problems just tumbled about me and grew heavier with each task;
"Why doesn't God help me," I wondered;
He answered, "You didn't ask."
I wanted to see joy and beauty, but the day toiled on, gray and bleak;
I wondered why God didn't show me—

He said, "But you didn't seek."
I tried to come into God's presence; I used all my keys at the lock.
God gently and lovingly chided, "My child, you didn't knock."
I woke up early this morning and paused before entering the day;
I had so much to accomplish that I had to take time to pray.
—Grace L. Naessens

As a teen, my testimony of prayer continued to grow. I remember one night at the beginning of my sophomore year of high school and I was preparing to go to a school dance—the first one of the year. I was a shy teenager and meeting new people was often scary for me, mainly because in my nervousness, I wouldn't know what to say.

I got dressed in a new outfit I'd found on sale at the mall, touched up my makeup, and felt extra happy I was having a good hair day. It was almost time to go. I exited the bathroom and went back to my bedroom to grab a sweater and say a prayer. Dusk was settling and a lamp cast the only beacon of light in the room. I knelt down by the side of my bed and my long hair fell around my face. I felt close enough to Heavenly Father; I could talk to Him about everything.

In my prayer, I asked Him to help me have a good time at the dance, be able to relax and be myself, and to travel in safety. On impulse I added, "Help me to meet someone who is right for now." When I stood up, I had no idea where *that* request had come from. I pushed it aside.

The high school cafeteria full of teenagers and a few scattered chaperones was bathed in subdued light. Loud music vibrated the air with its changing beat. I stayed by the entrance door scanning faces until I saw some of my friends and my apprehension suddenly lessened. The three of us sat down on the bench at a table with a good view of the dance floor. We were a little breathless with excitement, talking and giggling in hushed anticipation of what the evening would bring.

When the current song ended and a new one begun, someone tapped me on the shoulder. I turned and looked into the blue eyes of a young man with blond hair standing close to six feet in height. I had sensed him watching me earlier. He asked me to dance. I smiled with a flutter, accepted, and took his arm, and we walked toward an open space on the rapidly filling floor. I faintly recognized his face from passing in the hallways between classes, certain he was in a different grade. He introduced himself.

After the song was over he asked if we could sit and talk.

The rest of the evening seemed to pass in an instant. We got to know each other and danced several more songs. Through the following days and weeks we spent more time together and with each other's families. He wasn't LDS, but his standards were higher than some of the boys I knew that were.

I invited him occasionally to church on Sunday, as well as stake dances and mutual activities. He had many questions about the gospel; my own knowledge increased as I studied the scriptures to learn more I could share with him. He knew I was saving myself for a future husband who would take me to the temple.

The next fall, as a senior, he made the varsity football team. I went to all of his games. He took me to my junior prom but we both dated other people. The end of the summer, before he left for college, we went out one more time.

He had been the answer to my prayer from two years before. He helped me gain the self-confidence I needed at that time in my life and as I tried to set a good example as a member of the church, my own beliefs grew stronger.

Heavenly Father knows each of us so well, and He knows exactly what we need to be happy, grow, and learn in order to return home to Him.

A seminary teacher once suggested to her class that they spend at least fifteen minutes a day in personal prayer. Many of the students reacted with surprise. After class one of them approached her. The young woman expressed concern over being able to think of that much to say. The teacher asked her if she spent that much time, if not more, talking to her friends each day. The young woman replied, "Of course." The teacher challenged her to think about why she had more to talk to them about than she did with the Lord.

How can we know Him if we do not talk with Him? This scriptures reiterate this:

"How knoweth a man the master whom he has not served, and who is a stranger unto him, and is far from the thoughts and intents of his heart?" (Mosiah 5:13).

In *Teachings of Gordon B. Hinckley*, President Hinckley counseled, "The trouble with most of our prayers is that we give them as if we were picking up the telephone and ordering groceries—we place our order and hang up. We need to meditate, contemplate, think of what we are praying about and for and then speak to the Lord as one man speaketh to another."[1]

Don't we all lose interest quickly when we hear the same words repeated over and over? I know my children's eyes glaze with boredom when I remind them to brush their teeth or make their bed—if they even hear me tell them at all. It instantly creates a dead end conversation.

"Our prayers should be meaningful and pertinent. Do not use the same phrases at each prayer. Each of us would become disturbed if a friend said the same words to us each day, treated the conversation as a chore, and could hardly wait to finish it in order to turn on the TV and forget us."[2]

When praying to Heavenly Father:

"Go where you can be alone. Go where you can think. Go where you can kneel. Go where you can talk out loud to Him. Picture Him in your mind's eye as you pray. Control your thoughts so you think only about Him. Address Him as your Father and your Friend. Tell Him things you really feel like telling Him. Confide in Him. Ask Him for forgiveness. Plead with Him. Enjoy Him. Thank Him. Express your love and respect for Him. Listen for His answers."[3]

It was a scorching hot day in the middle of August when I pulled off the highway at the 7-Eleven gas station I regularly used. I was anxious to fill up the tank and return home to my air-conditioned house. I'd been running errands all morning and my energy was zapped from the heat.

At the first available pump I came to, I parked and shut off the engine. I retrieved a credit card from inside my purse and took the keys out of the ignition by habit, even though my nine-year-old son was in the car. He had come along to get a new pair of shoes for school.

While the gas was flowing smoothly into the tank, I washed the film of dust off the back window of my car.

"Mom, I'm so hot!" my son exclaimed, confirming his statement by wiping his damp brow with his hand and then on his gray plaid shorts.

"I know, bud. Me too. We're almost done." I could feel a new rivulet of perspiration begin to trickle down my back.

Two teenage boys came out of the mini-mart, each holding an extra large slurpee. One was colored blue, the other lime green. They laughed as they enjoyed a refreshing swallow of the frosty drinks on the way to their bicycles.

Click. The numbers on the gas pump stopped moving, announcing the total. I returned the pump handle to its proper place and took my receipt as soon as it popped out. When I got back in the car, I knew my son had been watching the two boys. He loved slurpees. I put the keys in the ignition and started the car.

"Son, would you like to get a slurpee before we head home?"

"Oh yeah!" he exclaimed. "Thanks, Mom."

I moved the car and reparked in front of the store. I pulled out two dollars from my wallet and handed them to him. "I'll wait here. Go ahead and get one." I nodded.

His eyes widened. "Aren't you coming with me?"

"No; you can go by yourself. You'll be fine. I can see you the whole time from here."

"But . . . I don't even know how the machine works. I can't do it myself. Can't you come?" His request was a small thing, but for some reason I felt prompted he should do it alone.

He hesitated, "I don't really need one . . . I guess."

"Son, I promise you can do it."

The wariness in his face hadn't left. I gave him an encouraging smile. He didn't return it with his own. Slowly he opened the door, got out, and looked at me. I gave him a thumbs-up. When he walked in the store I felt a little twinge of concern; it would have been so easy to go inside with him, help him get the treat, and pay for it at the register. I reminded myself of the feeling I had—this was a teaching moment.

When he came out of the store about five minutes later, he was grinning from ear to ear, holding his slurpee up like a trophy. "Hi, Mom," he said when he climbed in the car. He held out his hand. "Here's the change."

"You did it—great job! See it wasn't that hard."

He nodded sheepishly. "It was easy," he said then offered me a drink. I took a small one and felt it slide down my throat like ice. "Brr, that's cold." I shivered.

He laughed. "Do you want me to go get one for you?"

"No, thanks." I patted his shoulder. "You just enjoy yours."

Like I tried to teach my son to trust me, Heavenly Father teaches us to trust Him through our prayers. The more we pray, the nearer He becomes.

In the book of Alma, Alma headed a mission to Antionum, east of the land of Zarahemla where the apostate Zoramites were living. The Zoramites hadn't forgotten God completely, but they were not following the commandments and were only praying once a week in the synagogue, repeating the same words each time. After they went home, they spoke of God no more until they returned the following week. The poor who had helped build the synagogue were cast out because of their coarse apparel, and were labeled as filthy.

Amulek, one of the missionaries, taught the poor they could have God near them anyway, through continuous prayer.

> Therefore may God grant unto you, my brethren, that ye may begin to exercise your faith . . . that ye begin to call upon his holy name, that he would have mercy upon you.
>
> Yea, cry unto him for mercy; for he is mighty to save.
>
> Yea, humble yourselves, and continue in prayer unto him.
>
> Cry unto him when ye are in your fields, yea, over all your flocks.
>
> Cry unto him in your houses, yea, over all your household, both morning, mid-day, and evening.

> Yea, cry unto him against the power of your enemies.
>
> Yea, cry unto him against the devil, who is an enemy to all righteousness.
>
> Cry unto him over the crops of your fields, that ye may prosper in them.
>
> Cry over the flocks of your fields, that they may increase.
>
> But this is not all; ye must pour out your souls in your closets, and your secret places, and in your wilderness.
>
> Yea, and when you do not cry unto the Lord, let your hearts be full, drawn out in prayer unto him continually for your welfare, and also for the welfare of those who are around you." (Alma 34:17–27)

Heartfelt and sincere prayer brings Heavenly Father nearer to His children. Expressing gratitude for blessings and trials strengthens that bond.

NOTES

1 Gordon B. Hinckley, *Teachings of Gordon B. Hinckley* (Salt Lake City: Deseret Book, 1997), 469.

2 Ezra Taft Benson, *God, Family, Country* (Salt Lake City: Deseret Book, 1974), 121–22.

3 Bishop H. Burke Peterson, "The Miracle of Prayer," *Friend*, June 1974.

Chapter 3

A Grateful Heart

"In everything give thanks." —1 Thessalonians 5:18

"We must ask in prayer that God, by the power of the Holy Ghost, will help us see our blessings clearly even in the midst of our trials."[1]

It was the middle of December, and it looked it. Snow was steadily falling in the Salt Lake Valley and had been for several days. When I went to bed that night, snuggling close to my husband, I was glad to be in a warm house.

Later on something woke me up. I glanced at the clock by my bed; it was after three in the morning. I realized I hadn't heard my nineteen-year-old son come home. I whispered to my husband; he hadn't heard him either. I was worried; work never kept him out this late. I reached for my cell phone and sent him a text.

Are you okay?

No, he replied.

My heart started to pound. "*No*?" All kinds of thoughts started rushing through my head. I quickly showed my husband the message. He sat up in bed and immediately called.

Our son had been in an accident and had just barely gotten phone service again. He needed someone to come get him. My husband quickly got dressed, grabbed some warm blankets, and left.

He had been coming down the mouth of Little Cottonwood Canyon after his shift ended and unknowingly hit a patch of black ice. He lost control of his car and slid off the road hitting a concrete barrier. The front of the vehicle pointed up at a forty-five degree angle. Less than a foot off to the left was a twenty-foot drop into an icy creek.

The air bags had deployed causing minor injuries; he had been dazed but remained conscious. He told us he had fumbled around for his cell phone to call for help, but when he found it, there was no reception. Slowly, he had gotten out of the car, feeling shaken, and began walking down the road out of the mouth of the canyon. It was pitch black, bitter cold, and snowing hard. A mile and a half later, he found a small gas station and was able to use his phone.

The next forty-five minutes of waiting passed interminably slow. When I finally heard the garage door open, signaling my husband was back, I was filled with gratitude and relief. I met him as he came inside and immediately hugged my son close. He was tired, pale, and understandably upset about his car, but he was home safe. He asked for a father's blessing. After my husband finished, he was visibly calmer and able to go to sleep.

Before I went back to bed, I knelt down with a full and grateful heart and thanked my Heavenly Father. Earlier that day, worried over the weather, I had specifically said a prayer asking that my son would be safe traveling to and from work.

Some might argue with me, but I say my prayer was answered like many others before, and once again I was overwhelmed with gratitude.

"It is tempting to complain and murmur when life is challenging. . . . The act of thanking and praising has great power to help us endure and is one of the surest methods for increasing happiness. It is also a way to define our relationship with God, from whom all blessings flow."[2]

Several years ago I had the opportunity to attend Education Week at Brigham Young University. In one of the classes, we were challenged to start a gratitude journal; I accepted. I found a spiral-bound notebook with a pretty cover at a bookstore and began my first entry.

August 24—Today I returned home from BYU: what a wonderful and uplifting experience. Went to several classes, took notes, and felt the Spirit very strongly. I'm grateful Daryl watched the kids so I could go.

August 25—Today I spent several hours cleaning and organizing my home. I'm grateful for the beautiful home I live in and for my family. I'm also grateful my body is healthy and I can do things daily with energy and strength.

August 27—Today I spent most of the afternoon running errands. School starts tomorrow and I've been finishing up getting the children ready to go. We've been harvesting from our garden and I'm grateful my husband has such a "green thumb."

August 29—My youngest son turned ten today. He has taught me many things about patience. He is very loving. I'm grateful to be a mother.

Writing down the many blessings I have in my life has opened my eyes more clearly to how much Heavenly Father has given me and has increased my love and gratitude for Him.

When we are grateful, we recognize the good things in the world around us. Growing up in Alaska, close to the Chugach Mountains, I've enjoyed the rugged beauty no matter what the season: freshly white after a new snowfall, vibrant green in summer, golden orange in autumn. I've traveled the United States coast to coast, throughout Canada, Europe, and South America, and in each place I've found differences as well as uniqueness and beauty.

However, as our lives have become busier in this fast-paced world—full of modern conveniences, instant pleasure, and a plethora of diversions—sometimes its takes a child to remind us.

One young mother knelt beside her three-year-old and listened to his heartfelt bedtime prayer. He gave thanks for his big brother, for snow, for clouds, and for pizza. Humbled, she couldn't remember the last time she'd taken the time to give thanks for the simple blessings of life. She began to daily express her gratitude for those kinds of things and started seeing the world with fresh eyes. Her spirit was nourished and her heartaches and difficulties became easier to bear.

Acknowledging Heavenly Father for all the goodness around us doesn't mean we are blinded by rose-colored glasses. Evil is real, and there *is* opposition in all things. There is pain and suffering, and we're not immune to the darkness sin creates, but the light of Christ will always outshine it. Love will always be stronger than hate.

We must, "Fear not: for they that be with us are more than they that be with them" (2 Kings 6:16).

Elder Robert D. Hales once said that gratitude expressed to our Heavenly Father in prayer for what we have brings a calming peace. Peace can be hard to come by in today's world, but with God, it's possible.

Every day we're given contains 24 hours, 1,440 minutes, or 86,400 seconds.

Are we making the time to give God thanks?

JUST THINK . . . .

What if
God couldn't take the time to bless us today because
we couldn't take the time to thank Him yesterday?

What if
God decided to stop leading us tomorrow because
we did not follow Him today?

What if
we never saw another flower bloom because
we grumbled when God sent the rain?

What if
God didn't walk with us today because
we failed to recognize it as His day?

What if
God took away His message because
we failed to listen to the messenger?

What if
the door of the church was closed because
we did not open the door of our heart?

What if
God stopped loving and caring for us because
we failed to love and care for others?

What if
God would not hear us today because
we would not listen to Him yesterday?

What if
God answered our prayers the way
we answer His call to service?

What if
God met our needs the way
we give Him our lives?

—author unknown[3]

NOTES

1 Henry B. Eyring, "The Choice to Be Grateful," *Liahona,* December 2011.

2 Vaughn E. Worthen, "The Value of Experiencing and Expressing Gratitude," *Ensign,* March 2010.

3 "What If," www.inspirationalarchive.com/texts/topics/godsprovince/whatif.shtml.

Chapter 4

Pray Always

"Pray without ceasing." —1 Thessalonians 5:17

Not only should we pray when we're grateful, we should pray morning, noon, night, and anytime in between. Like Alma suggested, "let all thy thoughts be directed to the Lord" (Alma 37:36).

In the book *Prayer*, Elder Carlos E. Asay shared some things he'd learned while serving as a mission president. He decided he would "begin a series of interviews with the missionaries by asking, 'When did you have your last spiritual experience?'"

Some of the missionaries told him they hadn't "experienced anything special. Others said that it had been some time since they had felt [close] to the spirit," and others said they had "marvelous experiences" that very day or within a few days before.

"One missionary's answer, however, was unique. His response was, 'This morning.' Slowly, yet confidently, he replied, 'I prayed.'"[1]

Through prayer, we have the ability to feel peace and love and be close to Heavenly Father continuously.

One Friday evening in June, the sun was beginning to edge out of the sky. It was still warm, but a slight breeze softened the heat. The street was momentarily empty and I drank in the view from the porch of my border flower beds—yellows, pinks, whites, and purples mixed with vibrant green. The fragrance was sweet.

In the distance the sound of cars cruising down the freeway reminded me of the busyness of life, muted but close. It had been a long and challenging week caring for my husband and houseful of children—teenagers down to an eight-month-old daughter. In that rare few moments of respite, my spirit was enveloped in a comforting peace, and it was the perfect time to pray.

The scriptures teach us to "pray always" (Luke 21:36).

"Pray vocally as well as in thy heart; yea, before the world as well as in secret, in public as well as in private"(Doctrine and Covenants 19:28).

Modern-day leaders of the Church have also taught us to pray always.

"Carry . . . the spirit of prayer throughout every duty that we have to perform in life."[2]

We can pray when we are seeking safety or facing temptation, when we need guidance and inspiration—anytime we need help with anything.

A few years after moving to Salt Lake City, my stake was presented the opportunity to be part of the choir for the upcoming general Relief Society meeting in September. Eight women were chosen from the ward. It involved weeks of practices, but what an exciting opportunity! I couldn't say no.

The music was beautiful, and after each practice I came away spiritually uplifted. At one practice, the general Relief Society president spoke to us, and at another we heard from one of her counselors. New friendships were made, and the sisters in my ward formed a stronger bond.

When the day of the conference arrived, I had been fighting the flu and had been unable to keep much of anything down—I was weak. The night before my husband gave me a priesthood blessing, and I was promised through my faith I would be able to perform.

Several times that morning I ran back and forth to the bathroom while I tried to get ready. I curled my hair and put on my makeup while sitting on a chair in front of the mirror because of dizziness. My husband kept encouraging I could do it. With a prayer in my heart and feeling sick, I walked outside to meet my ride wondering how I could do it.

Inside the conference center, wearing our jewel-toned dresses, we were seated and the first practice began. I made it through the first song. When the second one started, I felt sure I was going to be sick to my stomach. I got up and shakily walked to the end of the row, praying I wouldn't throw up in front of everyone. One of the nearby staff led me to the infirmary where I lay down, missing the rest of the first practice, lunch, and all of the second practice.

I received another blessing, got some rest, and kept down a few saltine crackers—despite the nausea, I didn't have to race to the bathroom even once. That night I was able to perform with the choir, sitting down through all but the first song. It was an amazing experience to sit behind the prophet and other church leaders and hear our voices fill that great building with beautiful songs.

Literally within fifteen to twenty minutes after returning home I was back in the bathroom, being sick. The next few days were rough while I recovered completely, but I've always been grateful for that experience. I know the continuous prayers I pled throughout that day were answered, and despite feeling physically weak, I was given enough strength to perform to the best of my ability in that once-in-a-lifetime opportunity.

We can also pray when we're concerned for someone else—a friend or stranger—and we're even told to pray for our enemies.

One December, Christmas was less than two weeks away, and I was in a department store trying to finish up the rest of my shopping. I found the things I'd come to purchase and got in line to checkout, feeling relieved I could cross a few more items off my to-do list. The cashier was a middle-aged woman and she looked tired. She started to ring up what I had in my cart, and I asked her how her day was going.

"Today was supposed to be my day off," she told me with a sigh, "but I was called in because someone was sick."

I offered my sympathies.

"It's okay," she said, "I need the money. I have to get the windshield replaced on my car and new tires or I can't keep driving it." She hesitated, and added, "But I barely have enough to cover my rent this month. I'm not sure what I'm going to do."

I felt immediately humbled. I was buying Christmas presents and this woman was struggling to cover her basic needs. I wished I could help her. She finished bagging my items and I handed her the money.

"Good luck," I told her. "I hope you find a great sale on tires."

Her face lit up with a smile and she wished me a Merry Christmas. I headed to the car, still feeling sorry I couldn't do more. Then I realized I could—I could pray. I explained to Heavenly Father her situation and asked if He would help her get what she needed or send someone else that would.

When Jesus Christ appeared to the Nephites in America after His resurrection, He spent three days teaching them at the temple in the land of Bountiful. He taught in detail about prayer, including when to pray: "Therefore ye must always pray unto the Father in my name; and whatsoever ye shall ask the Father in my name, which is right, believing that ye shall receive, behold it shall be given unto you" (3 Nephi 18:19–20).

> [Pray] as we seek to learn gospel truths and then live them, as we seek his help in the major decisions of our lives, . . . involving schooling, marriage, employment, place of residence, raising our families, serving with each other in the work of the Lord, and seeking his forgiveness and continual guidance and protection in all we do. . . . As we gather together in prayer, whether in home, Church, social or public settings, we should remember the purpose of our prayers—to communicate with our Father in Heaven.[3]

NOTES

1 Carlos E. Asay, *Prayer* (Salt Lake City: Deseret Book, 1977), 43.

2 Donald W. Parry, "After This Manner . . . Pray Ye," *Ensign*, January 1996.

3 Spencer W. Kimball, "Pray Always," *Liahona*, March 1982.

Chapter 5

Yours, Mine, and Ours

"Pray in your families unto the Father." —3 Nephi 18:15

Not only should we pray always, we should also pray in different ways. Personal prayer, couple prayer, family prayer, public prayer—they're all needful and important at the appropriate times.

Daily personal prayer becomes natural and instinctive when we understand our true relationship with God—He is our father and we are His children. In the New Testament Jesus taught about our Heavenly Father's love for us.

"What man is there of you, whom if his son ask bread, will he give him a stone?

"Or if he ask a fish, will he give him a serpent?

"If ye then, being evil, know how to give good gifts unto your children, how much more shall your Father which is in heaven give good things to them that ask him?" (Matthew 7:9–11).

Eight-year-old Gilbert was new to cub scouts. At one of the den meetings he was given his first pinewood derby car kit with the instructions to go home and enlist the help of his dad. That night his dad was reading the paper, and Gilbert excitedly showed him the kit. His dad wasn't excited at all. Weeks passed and the kit remained unopened.

Finally, Gilbert's mom decided to help him. Lacking in carpentry skills, she read him the directions and encouraged him to get to work. He did and within a few days his car was finished. Despite its lopsided appearance, she was proud and so was he.

The night of the race arrived and Gilbert's confidence wilted as he looked at the other cars—painted to perfection with body styles built for speed. All the other dads had obviously helped. Some of the boys snickered when they saw Gilbert's, and to make things worse he was the only one there with just a mom.

The race began, and one by one the cars were eliminated. The final race was between Gilbert and the sharpest, fastest car. Before the buzzer went off Gilbert asked if they could stop for just a minute; he wanted to pray. He hit his knees holding his car. When he finished he stood with a smile and announced he was ready.

The owner of the other car stood by his dad as both cars sped down the ramp. Gilbert's car wobbled along gaining speed and won, crossing the finish line a fraction of a second before the other. He leaped into the air and yelled, "Thank you!" as the crowd roared in approval.

The Scout Master walked up to him, microphone in hand. "So you prayed to win, huh, Gilbert?"

"Oh, no, sir. That wouldn't be fair to ask God to help you beat someone else. I just asked Him to make it so I don't cry when I lose."[1]

Gilbert hadn't been there without a dad; his Heavenly Father was with him—just like He can be with us individually, in our marriages, and in our families if we ask.

"Couples as well as families and individuals need to remind themselves that putting themselves into a proper attitude to appropriately pray often supplies the necessary oil for the troubled waters of the day."[2]

In the book *A Man Called Peter*, Catharine Marshall writes of the power of prayer in strengthening a marriage: "Though like every normal couple Peter and I were sometimes in disagreement, we found that these differences could never become serious or bitter as long as we could pray together. So thoroughly did we learn this lesson that it was one of the chief bits of advice Peter always gave to couples whose marriages were almost bankrupt. 'If you will get down on your knees together,' he would tell them, 'your difficulties will soon be solved. You just can't pray together and stay mad at each other.'"[3]

I've become a better wife through prayer. It's amazing how quickly harsh or judging words can break the heart of someone we love. So many times I've wished I had simply kept quiet instead of saying something confrontational to my husband.

Angrily, I watched my husband's retreating back as he left the room. I hadn't finished making my point. I grabbed the nearest box of tissues and my purse and car keys. I couldn't stay in the house one more minute with him. Backing out of the garage, I nursed my wounded heart, wanting to scream out in frustration.

My mind raced with conflicting emotions as I drove. I hated the turmoil and wanted relief. I knew just the place to find it—along with a clearer perspective. The drive to the Bountiful Temple was roughly fifteen minutes from my home, a blessing I never took for granted, especially having lived over thirty years in Alaska without a single one.

I crested the hill, instantly invigorated by the sprawling view of the Valley and the Great Salt Lake beyond. As the brilliant white of the temple spires rose up in front of me, I released a deep calming breath. I pulled off the road, parked in front of the gates, and stared. The grounds were in full bloom. New tears coursed down my cheek. I grabbed another tissue, bowed my head, and started to pray.

"Dear Heavenly Father, I'm so upset with . . ." Silently I listed the complaints about my husband, holding nothing back. Each irritation I recited lightened the burden I'd felt. When I said all I needed to say, the Spirit began to teach. I had made mistakes too. An understanding of my husband was clarified, and the changes I needed to make in myself became evident. I ended my prayer with gratitude and the promise to do better.

Good marriages don't happen, they grow. One moment, one hour, one week, one month, one year, at a time.

President Hinckley has said, "I know of no single practice that will have a more salutary effect upon your lives than the practice of kneeling together as you begin and close each day. Somehow the little storms that seem to afflict every marriage are dissipated when, kneeling before the Lord, you thank him for one another, in the presence of one another, and then together invoke his blessings upon your lives, your home, your loved ones, and your dreams.[4]

Jesus Christ also taught the Nephites about the importance of family prayer.

"Pray in your families unto the Father, always in my name, that your wives and your children may be blessed." (3 Nephi 18:21)

It was dinnertime and my family was gathered around the table, hungry and ready to eat. The feeling in the dining room was not relaxed or carefree—it was tense. One of my children had been struggling in his interactions with family members and cross words had been spoken. That night was his turn to pray.

My husband called on him by name; everyone else sat silently and waited. Despite his sour mood, he didn't protest, folded his arms, and began to bow his head.

Suddenly he dropped his arms and looked abruptly up. "I can't," he said.

Four pairs of startled eyes focused on his.

He went on. "I don't feel the Spirit right now." He released a breath. "I need to get clear first." He started with an apology to his younger sister and continued until he had addressed everyone at the table. Some he talked a little longer to than others, but when he finished, the feeling in the room had changed. The tenseness had dissipated.

"I'm ready now," he announced and bowed his head. He started to pray, thanking Heavenly Father for each one of us, for his many blessings, and for the food we were about to eat. He asked that there would be no more contention in our home and we would feel love for one another. His words rang out warm and sincere.

The Spirit filled my heart in great abundance. I could see the rest of the family felt it too. Through my son's prayer our family unity was reinstated.

"I am sure that if we pray fervently . . . individually and as a family when we go to bed at night and when we arise in the morning, and around our tables at mealtime, we will not only be closer or more united as loved ones but we will grow spiritually through communion with our Heavenly Father."[5]

A kind father and loving husband passed away unexpectedly while at home. His youngest son found him. A medical team tried to resuscitate him, but it was too late. The mother was in a nearby city, and the older brother and sister were at work. Neighbors and friends of the family were called.

Soon the children gathered at the hospital with extended family while they tried to contact the mother. Once she arrived she was told of her husband's death and was taken to the small chapel in the hospital where her heartbroken children were waiting.

They rushed to be close to her, but before much was said, she told them to gather for family prayer. It was hard to comprehend just that morning their world had looked bright and now a tragedy had changed their lives. They knelt together, arm in arm, and prayed.

Comfort and strength wrapped around them. Their testimonies were reaffirmed, their hope was renewed, and love filled the family circle. Their father was gone but only temporarily, and they were an eternal family; someday they would be joyfully reunited again.

> There is no adequate substitute for the morning and evening practice of kneeling together—father, mother, and children. This, more than soft carpets, more than lovely draperies, more than cleverly balanced color schemes, is the thing that will make for better and more beautiful homes. . . . As together family members thank the Lord for life and peace and they all have. And as they thank the Lord for one another, there is developed within the family a new appreciation, a new respect, a new affection for another.[6]

Prayers in public set a tone of reverence in a group gathering. They are an expression of humility and show reliance and acknowledgment that God is and should be part of all we do. They should be direct, sincere, and appropriate, voicing gratitude, needs, and desires for those present. With matters of great concern, the combined faith of those in attendance can strengthen the supplications.

Three weeks into basic training, a group of fifty-six airmen were struggling to work as a team. One in particular recalled his mission and the power and unity that can come from praying with a companion. He approached the junior officers and requested permission to hold a nightly prayer meeting for anyone who wanted to participate. They agreed and were supportive.

At the first meeting, six airmen showed up. They read a few verses out of the New Testament relating to the challenges they'd been dealing with, then had prayer. Gradually their numbers increased. One airman that was asked to pray declined until a few weeks later. In that prayer, he asked for help for his family and strength for himself for the final weeks of training.

Later he reported the prayers for his family had been answered, and he had felt God with him during the rest of basic training. Reading the scriptures and seeing the example of the other airmen had helped him develop faith in God, where before he had none.[7]

Bruce R. McConkie once stated, "Prayer has a sanctifying effect; and it causes the blessings of heaven to be poured out; . . . we should pray for the success and triumph of all the programs of the Lord's earthly kingdom, and we should then suit our actions to our words."[8]

Our nation was founded on prayer and the Mayflower Compact. Written in November 1620, it begins with, "In the name of God . . . We having undertaken, for the glory of God . . . do by these presents solemnly and mutually in the presence of God, and of one another covenant and combine ourselves into a civil body politic."

Public prayer has aided the decisions of government leaders in times of war and peace. The Constitutional Convention of June 1787 had been meeting for weeks without agreement, when Benjamin Franklin rose to his feet and addressed President George Washington. He stated they had looked at models of government in ancient history and modern states without finding anything suitable for their circumstances.

"How has it happened, Sir, that we have not, hitherto, once thought of humbly applying to the Father of light to illuminate our understandings? In the beginning of the contest with Britain . . . we had daily prayers in this very room for divine protection."

He went on to request that "henceforth, prayers imploring the assistance of Heaven and its blessings on our deliberations be held in this assembly every morning before we proceed to business."[9]

The Apostle Paul seemed to indicate this in the scriptures, "supplications, prayers, intercessions, and giving of thanks be made for all men; For kings, and for all that are in authority; . . . this is good and acceptable in the sight of God, our Saviour" (1 Timothy 2:1–3).

NOTES

1 Author unknown

2 Marvin J. Ashton, Prayer (Salt Lake City: Deseret Book, 1977) , 81.

3 Catharine Marshall, *A Man Called Peter* (1951), 119–20.

4 *Marriage and Family Relations Instructor's Manual*, "Lesson 6: Strengthening Marriages Through Faith and Prayer."

5 Spencer W. Kimball, "Pray Always," *Liahona*, March 1982.

6 Gordon B. Hinckley, "The Blessings of Family Prayer," *Ensign*, February 1991.

7 Adapted from, Daniel Openshaw, "United By Prayer," *Liahona*, August 2007.

8 Bruce R. McConkie, *Doctrinal New Testament* (Salt Lake City: Bookcraft, 1973), 3:65.

9 *Prayer* (Salt Lake City: Deseret Book, 1977), 17:124.

Chapter 6

For Wisdom and Understanding

"Ask, and it shall be given you; seek, and ye shall find."
—Matthew 7:7

We're told in the scriptures, our Heavenly Father knows all things (2 Nephi 2:24) and through prayer He can enlighten our minds with wisdom and understanding. He's done that repeatedly for me.

Saying I was scared or nervous the first time I taught a lesson in Relief Society is putting it mildly. I'd taught in other callings I'd held in the Church, but teaching the women seemed overly intimidating. Thoughts of inadequacy were based on my own certainty that most of them had to be more qualified than I was.

Each day that passed, bringing me closer to the day of my lesson, my anxiety grew. I read the material over and over, made notes, studied the accompanying scriptures, and prayed, but I didn't feel ready. Something was missing.

Sunday was only a few days away, and I was waking up in the mornings with feelings of dread. I needed to pull myself together—my fears were getting overwhelming—and I knew the source was not God. I prayed again, asking for calmness, clarity of thought, and greater understanding on the subject of the lesson.

As I reviewed it again, two experiences from my own life came to my mind with a warm feeling of comfort. I had needed to make the lesson more personal. I always gained more from talks and lessons when true-life examples were given.

That was the beginning of the Lord guiding me to become a better teacher and public speaker. Being real and opening up a part of myself by sharing things I'd gone through and learned from created a much more meaningful connection with those in the class or congregation.

"That which is of God is light; and he that receiveth light, and continueth in God, receiveth more light; and that light groweth brighter and brighter until the perfect day" (Doctrine and Covenants 50:24).

Repeatedly through prayer I've received wisdom to handle situations in my life I wasn't dealing well with on my own, especially in my role as a mother.

My bedroom was quiet and warm from the afternoon sun, but I didn't find it comforting as I shut the door behind me. I was exhausted and filled with so much frustration I wanted to scream. I started to cry instead.

My son had lied to me again.

I had tried to do everything I knew how to get him to stop. Nothing worked. Not losing friends, video games, or television. Not writing sentences or doing dishes for a week. And none of the many talks or family home evening lessons we'd had about honesty seemed to make a difference. My discouragement ran deep and I had run out of ideas. How could I get him to understand the immense value of this principle? How could I believe anything he told me?

I'd prayed about it many times (at least I thought I had) in a general way, but the problem persisted and my discouragement and feelings of helplessness to change it increased.

I knelt down by my bed. The filtered rays of sunshine coming through the bedroom window warmed my back, and I started another prayer. I felt tired, sad, and at a loss of where to go next. "Father in Heaven, I don't know what to do. Please help me . . ."

I told him all of my concerns until my knees were sore. When I finished, I opened my eyes and grabbed a tissue to wipe the tears off of my face. I got up and sat on the edge of my bed. Releasing the emotions helped lighten my heavy heart, but I still didn't know what to do.

It wasn't long before a thought entered my mind.

Really, Heavenly Father, I questioned. *You want me to do that? How can that possibly work? What about the next time and the next time he tells me something?*

I was to tell my son I was not going to look back anymore at the times he'd been dishonest, the times he'd covered the truth with excuses or denials. That was over and done with. From then on, I would believe he was telling me the truth. I was going to trust him.

I called my son to my bedroom so we could talk and I told him right then I was drawing a line, separating the past from the future. I watched his eyes grow bigger as he listened. With parted lips, he searched my face.

"Unless you do or say something to break my trust, I am now giving it to you completely." *Heavenly Father, are you sure*? I asked again, feeling afraid.

His answer was a warm feeling of peace.

My son's eyes watered, and he hugged me. "Thanks, Mom. I love you." He turned and left the room.

My tears fell again.

Over the next several months I saw my son change. The first few times I asked if he was sure he was being honest or telling the truth, there was hesitation. Occasionally he changed his answers. As time passed the hesitations disappeared and his responses were strong and firm.

I would never have thought to handle that situation the way I did, on my own. That inspiration and guidance came directly from Heavenly Father as an answer to my prayers.

The Lord has promised to all the faithful: "If thou shalt ask, thou shalt receive revelation upon revelation, knowledge upon knowledge, that thou mayest know the mysteries and peaceable things—that which bringeth joy, that which bringeth eternal life" (Doctrine and Covenants 42:61).

A man who was raised in the Church became less active as a teenager. After serving in the military, he got married and had a family. One day his four-year-old daughter became ill and had to be put in the hospital. In desperation, and for the first time in many years, he knelt on his knees in prayer, asking that the life of his daughter be spared.

Her conditioned worsened. Gradually he sensed that his little girl would not live and his prayers changed; he no longer prayed for healing but rather for understanding. "Let thy will be done" was now the manner of his pleadings.

Soon his daughter was in a coma, and the father knew her hours on earth were few. Fortified with understanding, trust, and power beyond their own, the young parents prayed again, asking for the opportunity to hold her close once more while she was awake. The daughter's eyes opened, and her frail arms reached out to her parents for one final embrace—and then she was gone.

This father knew their prayers had been answered. A kind, compassionate Father in Heaven had comforted their hearts. God's will had been done, and they had gained understanding.[1]

"The object that our Heavenly Father has in requiring this [prayer] is that we may be in communication with Him, and that we may have a channel between us and the heavens . . . above . . . and in praying to God he will not only pray for light and the inspiration of His Holy Spirit, . . . but he will feel to thank God for the blessings he receives, realizing that life, that health, that strength, and that all the intelligence which he possesses comes from God.[2]

During the time the mother of a young man served as county treasurer, he spent a lot of time in her office. The office had a huge walk-in vault that hadn't been used for many years. One day while playing, he learned how to open it. When he told his mother, she didn't seem to think much about it.

Years later, his younger brother and a friend went with his mother to the office like he used to. Somehow the two little boys locked themselves inside the vault. When the mother discovered what had happened she tried but couldn't get it to open. The airtight vault only had enough oxygen inside to last a few hours.

Men with cutting torches, drills, and other equipment were called to come rescue the boys. The vault had been designed to resist any kind of forced entry and proved it was impenetrable. In desperation, the mother went into another room to kneel and pray. During her prayer, the time her older son told her he knew how to open the vault years before came back to her mind. Quickly, she rushed out of the building to get him from school.

On the way back to the vault, they tried to hurry past the crowds and uniformed rescuers, worried they'd be too late. Together they prayed he would be able to remember the combination—with God's help he did. When the huge vault door swung open, the workers and people in the crowds cheered and clapped.

Through prayer we gain inspiration to know what needs to be done in difficult situations. When the Lord enlightens our minds with wisdom, we can see the way to solve problems and do our best to accomplish His will.

The experience Joseph Smith had as a young boy while reading the Bible is a classic example of seeking wisdom and knowledge from God. Joseph wanted to join a church but didn't know which one was right. In his own words he wrote:

> At length I came to the conclusion that I must either remain in darkness and confusion, or else I must do as James directs, that is, ask of God. I at length came to the determination to "ask of God," concluding that if he gave wisdom to them that lacked wisdom, and would give liberally, and not upbraid, I might venture.
>
> So, in accordance with this, my determination to ask of God, I retired to the woods to make the attempt. . . . It was the first time in my life that I had made such an attempt, for amidst all my anxieties I had never as yet made the attempt to pray vocally. (Joseph Smith History 1:13–14)

Joseph did humbly seek an answer in prayer and the heavens were opened.

In the Book of Mormon, Nephi desired an understanding of the things his father, Lehi, had been teaching. He wanted to know for himself concerning the forthcoming destruction of the city of Jerusalem and why they had to leave their home and travel in the wilderness. He said: "Having great desires to know of the mysteries of God, wherefore, I did cry unto the Lord; and behold he did . . . soften my heart that I did believe all the words which had been spoken by my father"(1 Nephi 2:16).

"One of the greatest challenges facing us today is to develop sufficient wisdom, understanding, and inner strength so that we can live happily and successfully in our complex and difficult world and not be caught up in the mad scramble for the material things and pleasures."[3]

Asked for advice on more than one occasion by people who were successful in a material way, why they were still unhappy and confused, Elder Richards said the Lord already answered that question: "Seek not for riches but for wisdom, and behold, the mysteries of God shall be unfolded unto you, and then shall you be made rich. Behold, he that hath eternal life is rich" (Doctrine and Covenants 6:7).

NOTES

1 Adapted from H. Burke Peterson, "Adversity and Prayer," *Ensign*, January 1974, 18.

2 *Teachings of Presidents of the Church, Heber J. Grant*, 2002, 176.

3 Franklin D. Richards, "Seek Not For Riches But For Wisdom," *Ensign*, May 1976.

Chapter 7

Pleadings for Peace

"How oft shall my brother sin against me, and I forgive him?"
—Matthew 18:21

I thought I had already experienced the deepest heartache I could ever live through. A pain so intense it breathed within every cell, haunting my dreams then assaulting with clarity the moment I would awake. Its crippling effects made the mere thought of facing another hour dauntingly impossible, let alone another day.

I was wrong.

The source was different, but the anguish was as vibrantly strong and gut-wrenching as before, I couldn't believe how cruel life could be. The betrayal of a spouse is one thing; the betrayal of a child who once grew under my heart was quite another. The world around me became dreary and for a time I was unable to even feel sunlight penetrate my skin.

I struggled with bitterness. I was serving in a demanding leadership position in my ward that took hours away from my family. I felt like I was on-call 24/7 if one of the sisters had a crisis and they or the bishop needed me. How could I keep serving when I was barely functioning myself? Where were the promised blessings? The strength to do all I needed to do? Why was God letting this happen to me? Had I not already gone through enough?

All I ever wanted was to be a wife and a mother. My children were everything to me. From the moment I knew each of them were coming, I did whatever I could to help them have a healthy body, and when they were born, I was devoted to nurturing, teaching, and caring for them. I made mistakes, but I loved them fiercely.

I could not continue dwelling on the intensity of the hurt this son was creating in my life. I was close to the edge, and I knew it. My husband had been my "rock," but it was taking an obvious toll on him as well. I also had other children at home that needed me. I had to regain my ability to move away from the situation and function again. I had to let go.

I went to my Father in prayer and dropped my overwhelming burden at the Savior's feet. I couldn't carry it one second more and I told him so. The pain was taking away all that was good in my life and I had to let it go; it was a true test of faith. I asked Him to help me forgive.

His love for my son washed over me until it became one with my own. The hurt that had been crushing me was taken away, and peace and understanding flooded me with warmth. The desire to embrace my son and tell him I loved him was overwhelming. As tears flooded my eyes and poured down my cheeks, I was filled with light.

"As a wife, husband, parent, or loved one, you can feel compassion for one who is in the gall of bitterness from sin. Yet you should not take upon yourself a feeling of responsibility for those acts. When you have done what is reasonable to help one you love, lay the burden at the feet of the Savior. He has invited you to do that so that you can be free from pointless worry and depression."[1]

Christ's pure love can remove the blinders of resentment and hurt from our eyes, letting us view others the way our Heavenly Father does. None of us are free from faults, but the potential for greatness lies inside us all.

"Pray unto the Father with all the energy of heart, that ye may be filled with this love, which he hath bestowed upon all who are true followers of his Son, Jesus Christ . . . we shall be like him . . . that we may be purified even as he is pure" (Moroni 7:48).

In the inspiring book *The Hiding Place,* Corrie ten Boom shares the experience of meeting one of the guards from the German concentration camp she was imprisoned at years after World War II ended.

She saw him in a church in Munich, Germany, amid the crowd of people leaving the room where she had just finished speaking about forgiveness. He was bald, overweight, and wearing a dark gray overcoat, gripping his hat in his hands.

In a second she was back in a different place—Ravensbruck concentration camp. She and her sister, Betsie, along with others, were walking humiliated past the pile of shoes and dresses in the center of a large room. He wore a blue uniform and a cap on his head marked with a skull and crossbones.

Now he was approaching her.

> "You mentioned Ravensbruck in your talk," he was saying. "I was a guard there."
>
> He didn't remember her.
>
> "But since that time," he went on, "I have become a Christian. I know that God has forgiven me for the cruel things I did there, but I would like to hear it from your lips as well. Fraulein . . ." his hand came out . . . "will you forgive me?"
>
> She stood there as the memories washed over her. Her sister had died in that camp; how could this man erase her horrible death by just asking? Her hand stayed at her side while she struggled internally, a coldness clutching her heart.

"If ye forgive men their trespasses, your heavenly Father will also forgive you: But if ye forgive not men their trespasses, neither will your Father forgive your trespasses" (Matthew 6:14–15).

Corrie knew she had to do it, but she couldn't alone. She prayed for help. She relates:

> Woodenly, mechanically, I thrust my hand into the one stretched out to me. And as I did, an incredible thing took place. The current started in my shoulder, raced down my arm, sprang into our joined hands. And then this healing warmth seemed to flood my whole being, bringing tears to my eyes. "I forgive you, brother!" I cried, "with all my heart!" For a long moment we grasped each other's hands, the former guard

> and the former prisoner. I had never known God's love so intensely as I did then.[2]

Hidden wedges like hurt, anger, or pride do more damage to our selves than to those that inflict us with it, just like a misplaced faller's wedge did to a large tree.

A young boy working on his father's homestead found a discarded faller's wedge on their property. It was heavy—more than a foot long—and was used to bring down a tree. When inserted in a cut made with a saw and then hit with a sledgehammer, the cut gets bigger, eventually bringing down the tree.

The boy was late for dinner, something his mother didn't like, and decided he would lug the wedge to the shed later. He temporarily put it between the branches of a young walnut tree his father had planted near the front gate and planned to take care of it later. He forgot.

Years passed. The boy grew to be a man, and the walnut tree grew to be large. The man got married and eventually took over his father's farm. The wedge had become firmly imbedded and the tree healed over it.

The man grew old and his hair was completely white the winter the ice storm struck. There were wires down and accidents along the highway. The storm wasn't the worst one ever, but it was bad enough. During the cold night one of the three major limbs of the walnut tree split from the trunk and crashed to the ground. The top of tree became so unbalanced, it broke apart the rest. When the storm had ended, not even a twig had been left standing.

The next morning the farmer discovered the tree was in splinters across the ground. Dismay filled his heart when he discovered the forgotten wedge amongst the ruin. Normally a walnut tree of that size would have easily withstood the storm, but because the wedge had prevented the wood fibers in the branches from binding together completely, the tree had been lost.

"The Spirit must be freed from tethers so strong and feelings never put to rest so that the lift of life may give buoyancy to the soul. In many families there are hurt feelings and a reluctance to forgive. It doesn't really matter what the issue was. It cannot and should not be left to injure. Blame keeps wounds open. Only forgiveness heals."[3]

The only true source of lasting peace is the Savior himself. He has already felt and experienced everything we might. Through Him our hurt and pain can be lifted and taken away.

Where can I turn for peace, where is my solace?
When other sources cease to make me whole? . . .
He answers privately, reaches my reaching,
Gentle the peace he finds for my beseeching.[4]

As we face our own Gethsemane, we can be sure the Savior is our constant friend. His love is endless. His comfort is sweet. His kindness, freeing.

An older sibling looked to a younger brother as an example of honesty, kindness, faith, humility, and diligence. He was smart, on a good chosen career path, and would soon be marrying his sweetheart in the House of the Lord. It was horrible to find out he had been murdered. The emotional roller coaster seemed endless as the pain went on and on. How would he let it go?

The Atonement is not just for sinners, it is also for those who have been affected by the sins of someone else.

"Peace I leave with you, my peace I give unto you: not as the world giveth, give I unto you. Let not your heart be troubled, neither let it be afraid" (John 14:27).

"I, the Lord, will forgive whom I will forgive, but of you it is required to forgive all men" (Doctrine and Covenants 64:10).

He also promised His strength would sustain us.

"And I will also ease the burdens which are put upon your shoulders, that even you cannot feel them upon your backs, even while you are in bondage; and this will I do that ye may stand as witnesses for me hereafter, and that ye may know of a surety that I, the Lord God, do visit my people in their afflictions" (Mosiah 24:14).

NOTES

1 Richard G. Scott, "To Be Free of Heavy Burdens," October 2002.

2 Corrie ten Boom, *The Hiding Place*, 1971, Bantam Books.

3 Thomas S. Monson, "The Peril of Hidden Wedges," *Liahona* 2007.

4 Emma Lou Thayne, "Where Can I Turn For Peace," *LDS Hymns*, Salt Lake City, 1985.

Chapter 8

Instruments in His Hands

"Search diligently, pray always, and be believing."
—Doctrine and Covenants 90:24

I was traveling from Fort Rucker, Alabama, to Germany with an infant and a toddler by myself. My husband had left a few months previous on a military assignment and we had been waiting to join him until family housing was available. On the first leg of our journey, the flight was under an hour, but my baby cried the whole way. I wondered how I would survive the long hours ahead.

We switched planes and headed for Chicago to catch our international flight to Europe. I was grateful my baby slept this time, but due to airport delays and issues with the weather, we were late arriving. My connecting flight left in less than an hour, and I was starting to panic. The O'Hare airport has five different terminals and because I was coming in on a domestic flight and switching to an international one, the gate was a substantial distance away. I started to pray hard that we wouldn't miss our flight and I would know where to go.

When I got off the plane, I got the baby strapped in the stroller, settled my carryon and the diaper bag, and took my toddler's hand. I was quickly scanning signs as I made my way to the elevator, still not having a clue which direction to go. I could feel tears starting to build, and I kept praying.

One other person was on the elevator. He was clean cut and looked like a businessman. He glanced at my face and immediately asked, "Do you need some help?"

"Yes," I told him, "I need to get to the international terminal." I showed him the gate number on my boarding pass and the departure time.

"Wow," he said, wrinkling his brow "you're going to have to hurry." The elevator stopped. "You need to go this way," he pointed. I must have still looked confused. "I can show you," he offered.

I thanked him with relief, feeling the load on my shoulders lifted considerably. He offered to push the baby. We switched spots, I picked up my toddler, and we ran. I arrived at the gate breathless and flushed with only minutes to spare. The man handed me back the stroller with a smile. I thanked him again and he hurried away to catch his own flight.

I'm sure that man has long since forgotten about me, a young, stressed-out mother he helped in an airport over twenty-four years ago. But, I will never forget him—the person Heavenly Father sent to answer my prayer.

"God does notice us, and he watches over us. But it is usually through another person that he meets our needs."[1]

A former counselor in the stake presidency was asked by his employer to give a presentation to several regional salespeople from across the country, introducing their new marketing program.

He brought along several T-shirts he had collected from different areas of the United States, planning to hold one up at a time and ask the appropriate salesperson how the new program could help that area. He felt impressed to add one more that he originally passed over.

The presentation went well. When he reached the last shirt in the pile he briefly felt a wave of concern. It read "I'd rather be a Mormon." To his relief the group responded positively to a discussion about Salt Lake City. When he was ready to put the shirt down, he felt he should toss it to the salesperson from California, who was sitting in the second row. The man looked surprised as he caught it.

After the meeting he came up and asked him why he had thrown him that particular shirt. His simple response what that he felt he should. The man confided he'd been having a difficult year. He had been drinking a lot and traveling too much. His life was out of control and he'd joined Alcoholics Anonymous. Lately, he'd been feeling the next step was to embrace a religion. Last night in his hotel room, he felt good enough to pray and he asked God whether he should join the church he was raised in, his neighbor's church, or The Church of Jesus Christ of Latter-day Saints, which his wife was a member of. He felt good about the prayer but didn't feel like he had received and answer—until he caught the shirt.[2]

When we're in tune with the spirit, the Lord can prompt us to do or say certain things, even when we don't understand why. Those seemingly small things to us can impact someone else in a huge way.

Elder Russell M. Nelson was approached with a particularly difficult medical case, during the early pioneering days of heart surgery. A man requesting his expertise had suffered greatly. He came to him with high hopes Dr. Nelson would be able to help.

After a thorough exam and evaluation, it was discovered the man had two faulty valves, not the one he originally thought. One of the valves could be helped surgically, the other valve could not. Dr. Nelson told him surgery was not recommended. The man was disappointed.

Other visits ended with the same advice. He came again to speak with Dr. Nelson. In desperation and words full of emotion, he told him that he had prayed and been directed to come to him. He said the Lord would reveal to him how to repair the second valve and would make it known during the operation. He asked him to reconsider performing the operation and pray for the help he would need.

This man's faith had a great effect on Elder Nelson and he didn't know how he could turn him away again. They prayed together, and he agreed to try. He prayed repeatedly for direction as the time for the surgery grew closer but still wasn't getting answers as to what he should do. When the surgery started, he still didn't know.

He fixed the first valve and then moved on to the second. It was intact but dilated so badly it was no longer functioning. While he examined it, a distinct message filled his mind of what needed to be done. He announced it to his assistant, but they weren't sure how to go about it.

Then a detailed picture came to his mind with dotted lines where the sutures needed to be placed. The complete repair was diagrammed. The surgery was a success.

The patient recovered rapidly, and not only was he helped but also a procedure to help others with similar problems had become possible. Heavenly Father had answered their prayers.[3]

"When filled with God's love, we can do and see and understand things that we could not otherwise do or see or understand. Filled with his love, we can endure pain, quell fear, . . . renew strength, and bless and help others in ways surprising even to us."[4]

I was sitting in sacrament meeting feeling emotional and overwhelmed by difficult challenges I currently faced. That morning I'd been tempted to stay home and wallow in self-pity. I wasn't up to pasting on my "Sunday Smile," I rationalized. Besides, I would commit to spend extra time studying my scriptures; surely that would be just as spiritual.

I didn't consider it for long, despite how tempting it was. I needed to get up and go at least for my children's sake. Staying home without being sick would not be the best example. I got ready for church and even with my slow start we made it on time. Relief Society was good as always, and in Sunday School we were studying the New Testament, one of my favorite books of scripture. I never tire of learning about the Savior and His life. Still, my problems weighed heavily.

After the sacrament was blessed and passed, it was time for testimonies. A few young children in the ward went first, their words eliciting a ripple of chuckles through the congregation—it was hard to join in. I glanced at the clock, disappointed to see how little time had passed and then felt a stab of guilt for being impatient. I was where Heavenly Father wanted me to be.

The next person to stand up was a young man who had recently returned from his mission. The story he proceeded to share seemed to be meant just for me. The Spirit touched me and I was flooded with warmth and hope. Truths I had known but forgotten quickly filled my mind and tears pricked my eyes. I felt light. My gratitude toward this young man for sharing his testimony linked with my gratitude for my Heavenly Father—thank goodness I hadn't stayed home.

If we trust in the Lord and remain obedient even when it's not easy the blessings will come, often in unexpected ways. When He needs us and we're listening, we can be the answers to others' prayers, and often, others are the answers to ours.

A friend shared the following:

> A woman with whom my family had been close for many years, lay dying in bed. She had been ill for a long time and had lost the ability to move. My husband and I were asked to come and visit and offer what comfort we could to the family.
>
> Her husband and two sons were present when we arrived. After my husband offered a special prayer on her behalf, I felt this feeling that I should hug the youngest son. I pulled him into a hug, and then eventually we left.
>
> Three days later she died, and my husband and I returned to pay our final respects and again offer comfort to the family. The youngest son arrived shortly after we did. At that time, I took him to the side and I told him that I had felt the impression the last time we were there that his mother had wanted me to give him a hug.
>
> He began crying and said that he had been praying that he would receive some sign that she loved him.

"And this is the blessing which hath been bestowed upon us, that we have been made instruments in the hands of God to bring about this great work" (Alma 26:3).

NOTES

1 Spencer W. Kimball, "The Abundant Life," *Ensign*, July 1978.

2 Adapted from, Ron Holmes, "The Answer That Fit: Mormon Journal," 1995.

3 Adapted from, Russell M. Nelson, "The Sweet Power of Prayer," *Ensign*, April 2004.

4 John H. Groberg, "The Power of God's Love," *Ensign*, November 2004, 11.

Chapter 9

How He Answers

"My sheep hear my voice." —John 10:27

John Burroughs, a naturalist, was walking through a crowded park one summer evening. Above the sounds of the city he heard the song of a bird.

He stopped and listened. Those with him hadn't heard it. He looked around. No one seemed to have noticed.

It bothered him that everyone missed something so beautiful.

He took a coin from his pocket and flipped it in the air. It hit the concrete with a ring, no louder than the song of the bird. Everyone turned; they could hear that.

Like the song of the bird amid a city of sounds, answers to our prayers in the noisy confusion of the world can be easy to miss—unless we're tuned in. I've often received answers to my prayers or a prompting of something I need to do in the early hours of the morning. I wake up—not completely—but because it's quiet and my mind is calm, I can hear.

Other times an answer comes as a feeling—a warm rush inside, confirming truth or a warning—or a thought or idea of understanding or direction to help someone else. It can also come as pure intelligence flowing into us, giving us "sudden strokes of ideas."[1]

"Delicate, refined spiritual communications are not seen with our eyes, nor heard with our ears. And even though it is described as a voice, it is a voice that one feels, more than one hears . . . the spirit does not get our attention by shouting or shaking us with a heavy hand. Rather it whispers. It caresses so gently that if we are preoccupied we may not feel it at all."[2]

Sometimes an answer will come when we are studying the scriptures. We are encouraged to "feast upon the words of Christ; for behold, the words of Christ will tell you all things what ye should do" (2 Nephi 32:3).

I've also had experiences when I've been struggling with something or I'm feeling the buffetings of the adversary, and even though I may not be currently reading my scriptures, an answer in the form of a scripture I've read previously comes clearly to my mind, and immediately I feel peace.

In the Doctrine of Covenants we learn, "Yea, behold, I will tell you in your mind and in your heart, by the Holy Ghost which shall come upon you and which shall dwell in your heart" (Doctrine and Covenants 8:2).

The closer we come to our Heavenly Father by obeying the commandments, having faith, and doing our best to follow our Savior's example, the easier it becomes to receive and discern answers to our prayers.

Sometimes there isn't a clear-cut yes or no answer because either choice could be fine, or maybe we will receive a greater understanding to solve the problem ourselves.

"It is not the usual purpose of prayer to serve us like Aladdin's lamp, to bring us ease without effort. Often the purpose of prayer is to give us strength to do what needs to be done, wisdom to see the way to solve our own problems, and the ability to do our best in our tasks."[3]

A woman went to the Lord for an answer concerning a man she was thinking about marrying. She met him as a sophomore in college and they shared many interests and goals, including wanting a temple marriage and a family, but there were some differences that could be problematic in a future together.

When he proposed, she took his ring. Later she gave it back and then accepted it again with mixed feelings. She prayed hard for an answer confirming her decision, wanting a "burning in her bosom," or a "stupor of thought." Neither came. She continued to pray, many times and in different places asking that she would know the right thing to do.

Still there was no answer. She felt confused, abandoned, and wondering if she lacked enough faith.

Twenty-one months after she met him, they were married in the temple without her knowing for certain it was right. She made the decision on her own, and committed despite the risks she knew were there. What she came to learn was the Lord was teaching her a different lesson.

She had wanted God to guarantee her a good relationship with the man that would be her husband. Instead, He expected her to solve the problems and make the commitment on her own. In the process, she and her husband grew closer and she experienced personal growth as well. The Lord knew that was what she needed.

> What do you do when you have prepared carefully, have prayed fervently, waited a reasonable time for a response, and still do not feel an answer? You may want to express thanks when that occurs, for it is evidence of His trust. When you are living worthily and your choice is consistent with the Savior's teachings and you need to act, proceed with trust . . . when you are living righteously and are acting with trust, God will not let you proceed too far without a warning impression if you have made the wrong decision.[4]

I struggled greatly with a decision regarding where one of my children should go to receive the best help at a critical time in his life. I researched, I prayed, I fasted, and I received priesthood counsel, but when I felt like one place in particular had what my son needed, I was filled with a stifling darkness that confused me greatly. My heart was heavy and weighed down with discouragement. When the time to make a final decision was at hand and I could not receive a peaceful confirmation, I felt panicked.

I was in tears the afternoon I made a long-distance call to my mother—a trusted source of comfort and wisdom I'd turned to all throughout my life. I shared what I'd been experiencing, relaying the steps I'd taken in searching for an answer as well as all the reasons my husband and I felt the particular place was the right one for our son to go.

She listened without interrupting until I finished. When I asked her what she thought I still needed to do, she told me it sounded like I had already done what was required. A feeling of disappointment touched me; I had expected something more.

Our conversation grew quiet as I pondered on her words, still wondering how to move forward with the critical situation. It was then understanding hit.

It was the right place.

The doubts and pressing feelings of darkness I'd been battling were coming from the adversary—he knew it was right too. Life-changing miracles were in store for my son, and he didn't want them to happen.

Making the best choice and moving ahead took faith, and the peace I wanted didn't come instantly, but the blessings from a loving Heavenly Father have been beyond our expectations.

It has been said, before the advent of something good and great, Satan always works to prevent it.

"The nearer a person approaches the Lord, a greater power will be manifested by the adversary to prevent the accomplishment of His purposes."[5]

When Heavenly Father answers our prayers with a yes, we feel confident. When he answers no, we must trust he is guiding us from making mistakes. When an answer doesn't come when we want it, our faith will grow when we take accountability and act on a decision consistent with His teachings.

If the decision we've made is right, we will feel good and things will fall into place. If not, He will let us know before we go too far.

"I will tell you in your mind and in your heart, by the Holy Ghost" (Doctrine and Covenants 8:2).

"Behold, thou knowest that thou hast inquired of me and I did enlighten thy mind; and now I tell thee these things that thou mayest know that thou hast been enlightened by the Spirit of truth" (Doctrine and Covenants 6:15).

"If you desire a further witness, cast your mind upon the night that you cried unto me in your heart, that you might know concerning the truth of these things. Did I not speak peace to your mind concerning the matter?" (Doctrine and Covenants 6: 22–23).

When Nephi was commanded to obtain the brass plates from Laban back in the city of Jerusalam, his response was, "I will go and do "(1 Nephi 3:7).

He acted.

Twice he was unsuccessful, but he didn't quit. "I was led by the Spirit, not knowing beforehand the things which I should do. Nevertheless I went forth" (1 Nephi 4:6–7).

He practiced faith and didn't give in to discouragement. Through inspiration he eventually was led step by step, "given . . . power [to] accomplish the thing which the Lord hath commanded" (1 Nephi 5:8).

In Europe at the end of World War II, a young woman and her parents were sitting at their kitchen table one evening and heard a loud disturbance. They discreetly looked out and saw the streets of their village filling with enemy troops from two directions, some riding motorcycles and driving trucks and tanks. She was afraid.

Her faithful father calmly told his family not to be scared, and suggested they should kneel down and pray for protection. In that prayer, he asked that their home would become invisible to the approaching soldiers. When he finished praying, the mother prayed, and then the young woman prayed.

They returned to the table, watching cautiously out the window. Soldiers invaded every house on the street; theirs was the last house at the end. The soldiers approached their home but went passed and continued to the next street. The family saw them enter every house in their view from their window.

The invasion went on for close to two hours before a loud whistle was blown. The soldiers returned to their vehicles and left. The family knelt again this time in gratitude and offered prayers of thankfulness for being protected.

The next day they found out from a friend about the horrible things the soldiers had done inside the houses. She was stunned to find out the soldiers had not come to their house. They were the only ones in the area that had been left alone.

Whether Heavenly Father answers our prayers right away or our patience and faith are tested while we wait, we can find peace by trusting they will be answered at the perfect time—His.

NOTES

1 *Teachings of the Prophet Joseph Smith*, 151.

2 Boyd K. Packer, "The Candle of The Lord," *Ensign*, January 1983, 52–53.

3 Richard L. Evans, *The Man and the Message* (Salt Lake City: Bookcraft, 1973), 289.

4 Orson F. Whitney, *Life of Heber C. Kimball* (Salt Lake City: Bookcraft, 1967), 132.

5 Richard G. Scott, "Recognizing Answers to Prayer," *New Era*, August 2003.

Chapter 10

His Timing, Not Ours

"And he prayed again, and the heaven gave rain, and the earth brought forth her fruit." —James 5:18

A few years ago my oldest daughter announced her engagement. Ever since she was a young girl, she had asked me to make her wedding dress—the time had arrived.

We were both excited the day we went shopping to our favorite fabric store to begin the important task. She had previously tried on dresses at several bridal shops and knew the style and fit she liked best.

We both loved her final choice. It was a Vogue pattern—a bit complicated but beautiful. I had sewn a variety of clothing for many years, including the dress I wore to my high school senior prom; however, this dress was more elaborate by far. Admittedly I had a moment or two of self-doubt then a calm reassurance came over me. I knew I could make it with Heavenly Father's help.

My least favorite part of sewing is cutting out the fabric and this dress had more pieces than anything else I'd ever made. I spent a good two days cutting, earning an unwanted backache and sore hand. What a relief it was when I was done. The following week I started to sew and then the real adventure began.

The bodice of the dress had five layers. I made a practice one out of muslin according to my daughter's measurements. It was way too big. The next one I made two sizes smaller, it was still too big. The third time around I was wondering what I would do if it still wasn't right and felt discouraged, doubting my abilities to get the custom fit she wanted. However, I knew I had to continue on; my daughter was counting on me.

When the bodice was ready for her to try on, my stomach was in knots. If this one didn't fit, I would need to buy new fabric and start completely over. Not a pleasant thought. She got it on and it looked okay—so far so good. I was starting to feel optimistic. The true test would be after the zipper was in. The pattern called for an invisible zipper which would be on the side of the bodice. That in itself was a bit intimidating. I reread the directions several times making sure I was doing it just right.

My attempt was sincere, but even then I had to unpick one side two times. Again, the third time was a charm! The zipper went in wonderfully and I was so relieved. Then we had another fitting. When I moved the zipper tab upward to close the gap between the two sides I felt a shudder of dread. It didn't look like it would close. When it did I was worried she couldn't breathe.

She looked in the mirror and squealed with delight. "It's perfect Mom! Oh thank you!"

"Are you sure it isn't too tight? What about here?" I pointed to her waist, still not feeling for certain it was right.

"No, it fits great!" She shifted the bodice. "See, I still have a little wiggle room." She grinned.

I let the breath escape I had been holding. All I had left was the inner lining and the skirt. I figured I was home free. Not quite. The dress had a train and draped to one side in the back with swirls of white chiffon. I sewed and unpicked, and sewed some more and unpicked again. It just wasn't laying right. I was frustrated and tired of unpicking seams. More than once I had the thought I would like to drop the dress on the sewing table and walk away. It was taking me so much longer than I had expected.

The rest of the week I spent every day sewing and every other room in my house looked like it. My family was also forgetting what eating a well-balanced meal was like. Quitting was very tempting. I thought about calling in a few favors from a friend who was an excellent seamstress, thinking maybe she could take over. I knew in the long run I would regret that.

So I kept at it. And finally the skirt was on and it actually looked like a dress. When my daughter tried it on, I was in awe—it fit her so well and draped just perfectly. Did I really make that?

The dress was strapless, so the last step was making a bolero jacket. I cut out the fabric and lining in her size and thought this part of the dress would be a piece of cake. The pattern was fairly simple. It ended up much more time consuming than I was expecting. I had to mend a few spots where the chiffon was fraying, make the seams more narrow to add some extra room, and because I sewed the lining to the inside bottom of the sleeves it wouldn't turn completely right side out. I discovered that part of the sleeves had to be hemmed by hand—more unpicking.

When my daughter tried it on, it looked okay. She couldn't raise her arms very far; it was a little tight across the shoulders. She said it was fine; she would adjust during the dancing at her reception. I was more than ready to be finished, make do, and ignore the flaws. I mulled it over. The next day I knew I had to make another one, one that fit better and was more comfortable.

I hoped this time it would go quicker, since I'd made one already. I still spent most of the day on it. Once it was done, she tried it on again with the dress. It looked much better and she was happy she could move her arms without it pulling. I had her turn from all sides, looking for any puckers or spots that needed to be readjusted. I couldn't find any. She looked beautiful—I had done it!

I thought back over the last few weeks, the times I wanted to quit, or the times I felt like leaving something instead of fixing it. The frustration I dealt with in dealing with the slippery chiffon and having to recut the fabric more than once on some of the pieces. There were white threads of different sizes all around me from unpicking, more than I ever have when I sew. The experience of making her wedding dress reminded me of an important lesson.

How many times in life when we're facing difficult challenges are there days we sometimes get tired of pressing forward? How often do we want it to get better right now? Giving up is enticing and an easier road often beckons. Do we wonder if our prayers for help are bouncing of the ceiling, and rationalize its okay to quit; we've done what we could?

I wanted to quit several times, cut corners, or scream in frustration as I sewed. The result of not giving up was a beautiful dress—a dress for one of the most significant days of my daughter's life, a dress she would cherish always. How much greater is the reward, the satisfaction and sense of accomplishment, the elation of giving something hard everything we have and succeeding? How much greater are the refining lessons we learn along the way? If we give up before we reach the goal, are we sacrificing an important part of who we can become?

Heavenly Father knows us much better than we know ourselves. When the heavens seem silent and we grow weary of petitioning the Lord, we might wonder if we've been abandoned. We might feel scared, uncertain, or even angry. Waiting, wondering, and trying to move ahead is a trial of faith and holding onto that faith is actively trusting in Him regardless of what happens.

The turning point comes when we surrender our will to His. When we remember He loves us purely and completely, and whatever happens will be in our best interest, we can let go.

President Hinckley once said, "Kneel in prayer before the Almighty with thanksgiving unto Him for His bounteous blessings . . . then stand on your feet and go forward as sons and daughters of God to bring to pass His eternal purposes, each in your own way."[1]

One young man, a brilliant student for whom school had always been easy, struggled when he entered the Missionary Training Center before going to serve a mission in Peru.

> He found the Spanish language impossible. He studied, he worked, he fasted, he prayed; but Spanish remained an alien obstacle. One day a friend found him sitting on the stairs, head in his hands and tears on his face. "What more can I do to learn the language and be a good missionary?" he asked.
>
> Several months later, his mother said to him, "I'm sorry you've had such a hard time with the language."

> "No," he replied, "be glad for it. If God had answered my first prayers, I wouldn't have developed the relationship I now have with Him. The struggle has given me humility and faith and strength of testimony I never had before."[2]

The scriptures are full of examples of waiting for the Lord's time. In Doctrine and Covenants we read about the prophet Joseph Smith struggling greatly, while he and several others waited to be released from Liberty Jail. At one especially low moment, he cried out, "O God, where art thou? And where is the pavilion that covereth thy hiding place? How long shall thy hand be stayed, and thine eye, yea thy pure eye, behold from the eternal heavens the wrongs of thy people and of thy servants, and thine ear be penetrated with their cries?" (Doctrine and Covenants 121:1–2).

In Doctrine and Covenants 122:7, the prophet's prayers were eventually answered and he was taught at the same time, "All these things shall give thee experience, and shall be for thy good."

In the Bible, we learn Jacob waited seven years to marry Rachel. Elizabeth and Zacharias waited much longer for a child. For forty years, the children of Israel waited in the wilderness before they could enter the Promised Land.

I love the story in the Book of Mormon about the two thousand stripling warriors. Helaman led them in battle against the Lamanites under the direction of Captain Moroni. Near the end of the book of Alma, Helaman wrote an epistle to Moroni, updating him on what had been happening.

They had had many successes. By the time they reached the city of Manti, the Lamanites had reinforced their strongholds and were much more numerous than them. Before they could try and conquer the city they needed more strength and provisions, so Helaman sent a request to the governor and then they waited for help to arrive from Zarahemla. Meanwhile, the Lamanite armies continued to fortify themselves.

Helaman and his men waited in the difficult circumstances for many months, and it got to the point they were almost out of food.

> The cause why they did not send more strength unto us, we knew not; therefore we were grieved and also filled with fear. . . . Therefore we did pour out our whole souls in prayer to God, that he would strengthen us and deliver us out of the hands of our enemies, yea, and also give us strength that we might retain our cities, and our lands, and our possessions, for the support of our people. . . .
>
> Yea, and it came to pass that the Lord our God did visit us with assurances that he would deliver us; yea, insomuch that he did speak peace to our souls, and did grant unto us great faith, and did cause us that we should hope for our deliverance in him. And we did take courage . . . and were fixed with a determination to conquer our enemies. (Alma 58:9–12)

Eventually, they did receive food and more men to help them, and even though their numbers were still much smaller than that of their enemies, they were able to conquer the city of Manti with the Lord's help. Not one soul was lost.

Helaman didn't know why they had to wait so long for assistance. He and his men were afraid and grieving, but they didn't lose faith. They continued to pray for strength and deliverance and it did come, but in the Lord's time.

I've had experiences in my own life when I've felt the heavens were silent and my faith has been tested. But each new day as I continued to be obedient, to be patient, and to trust Heavenly Father, eventually the guidance or answers I was seeking came.

This scripture has helped me keep things in perspective: "peace be unto thy soul; thine adversity and thine afflictions shall be but a small moment; And then, if thou endure it well, God shall exalt thee on high; thou shalt triumph over all thy foes" (Doctrine and Covenants 121:7–8).

Recently, I faced a horrible crisis situation in my family. It went on for days, weeks, and months and I didn't know how much longer I could take it. I spent many times on my knees in prayer, I fasted, I counseled with priesthood leaders and medical professionals, I attended the temple regularly, and I studied and read to better understand what we were dealing with.

After an especially bad day, I knelt down on my knees and sobbed, feeling completely discouraged, overwhelmed, and close to despair. I felt I'd done all I could, and I pled with God, harder than ever before to send help.

Things became worse, and one night it all came to a head and drastic measures became inevitable. My heartache grew making such hard decisions, and those next couple of weeks I hurt, worried, questioned, and cried even more. But that night, unrecognized at first, the turning point had come.

Slowly, little miracles began to happen. Glimpses of light broke through the darkness and my trust in the Lord was strengthened again. We had never been alone, even though during the scary times it felt like it. During stake conference, the stake president was discussing adversity, and in his Sunday talk I was pierced by his words, as if he were speaking directly to me.

He said that sometimes when we are in the midst of a crisis, we may be praying, fasting, reading our scriptures, going to church—doing all we can to be obedient and strong—but the Heavens are silent. In reality, Heavenly Father is there, but sometimes He pulls back to test our faith. Will we continue to be obedient and strong or will we give up and turn away from Him? When we don't give up, the miracles start to happen and the blessings come.

The warmth of the Spirit flooded my heart, confirming it was true. It's difficult to have patience and trust God's timing, but when we do, it's so worth it.

"I waited patiently for the Lord; and he inclined unto me, and heard my cry. He brought me up also out of an horrible pit, out of the miry clay, and set my feet upon a rock, and established my goings. And he hath put a new song in my mouth, even praise unto our God: many shall see it, and fear, and shall trust in the Lord" (Psalm 40:1–3).

I recall a talk where President Uchtdorf related a personal experience in a recent conference address when he was preparing to be trained as a fighter pilot. They spent a great deal of time running and training physically. He mentioned not understanding why seemingly endless running was of such great importance to fly a plane.

As he ran, he did notice something that bothered him. Regularly men who smoke, drank, and engaged in other things contrary to the gospel passed him by. He found that frustrating to understand especially based on the promise of the Word of Wisdom that when followed, one could run and not be weary. He definitely was weary; how could these others with different standards not be? He wondered whether that promise really was true.

An answer did not immediately come. It wasn't until years had passed he saw the blessings from obeying the Word of Wisdom. He also recognized that spiritual blessings can come instantly from obedience to God's laws.

We all have times in our lives we must be patient and wait. I remember being pregnant with my first baby. I was so excited to hold that precious baby in my arms. It had been a difficult pregnancy; unfortunately, the bathroom and I became intimate friends as I repeatedly lost the content of my stomach several times a day. I had no idea I could feel so sick for so long. As my due date approached, my anticipation grew. It came and went, then a day passed, then another, and another until soon a week had gone. Then a new one began and the days continued to pass—and still no baby.

I seriously questioned if I would be pregnant forever, knowing of course I wouldn't be; it just felt like it. Those days dragged by more slowly than anytime I had ever experienced before, and I pled some heartfelt prayers that the waiting would quickly end. Phone calls from anxious friends and family wondering if I had any news only made things worse. I couldn't believe it was possible for one hour, let alone another day to slip by at such an exhaustive pace. The day I hit my two-week mark, my doctor decided to induce labor. Early that morning before the sun was up, he met us at the hospital and broke my water. Afterward he encouraged me to get up and start walking in hopes contractions would begin.

Together my husband and I trudged the corridors of that hospital floor. In stocking feet and wrapped in a bathrobe with my huge belly sticking out in front, I began that final journey of birthing our son. My spirits were high. The first hour or two my husband and I softly talked and laughed about the life-changing event finally so close to happening.

When the third hour began and I still hadn't had a contraction, my smile had dimmed.

Back in the room we met with the doctor and agreed it was time to start me on an IV with pitocin. The waiting continued all through the day and into the night until finally, when the time was right, our sweet baby entered the world.

I realized my son was born when he was supposed to be. I didn't know why the specific day was so important, but trying to change it didn't happen regardless of my impatience. That experience taught me sometimes enduring the waiting is all we can do. God's timing is often different from ours and He expects us to trust Him in faith.

"We cannot have true faith in the Lord without also having complete trust in the Lord's will and in the Lord's timing. As a result, no matter how strong our faith is, it cannot produce a result contrary to the will of Him in whom we have faith. . . . Trust in the Lord's will and in the Lord's timing. . . . Remember that when your prayers do not seem to be answered in the way or at the time you desire."[3]

A man sat alone in his small trailer, on a stifling August day. He couldn't remember ever feeling so miserable, hot, hopeless, and destitute. He recently lost his business, his home, his wife of eighteen years to divorce, and his children.

Months earlier he had moved to Las Vegas to find work. He was hired, but things didn't go well, and he lost the job. That was the final blow. Alone and in a strange city, he was financially broke and brokenhearted. He knew he should turn to Heavenly Father, but he felt unworthy.

In his trailer, the anguish he had submerged for many months forced its way out, and he began to sob uncontrollably, crying aloud. "My wife has thrown me out. My boss has thrown me away. I have no way of knowing that Thou hast not also discarded me as useless." He wept to Heavenly Father that he was unable to feel His love or comfort through his barrier of grief and that he needed Him that very hour.

God works in His own way and in His own time. In that instance, his timing aligned with His. He had scarcely finished drying his eyes when there was a knock on his trailer door—the first in the time he had lived there. Standing in front of him was his priesthood leader and two assistants.

He invited them in and told them about his job situation. The high priest group leader sensed he might need a priesthood blessing. He didn't share in detail what he had just been through or that they were an answer to prayer, but the inspired priesthood leader used words of promise relating to his plea twenty minutes before.

Heavenly Father had not tossed him aside. He would help him be refined and proven through his trial because He loved him. His despair was replaced by a quiet sense of peace and assurance of God's care.[4]

"For he will give unto the faithful line upon line, precept upon precept; and I will try you and prove you herewith" (Doctrine and Covenants 98:12).

If we put our faith in the things of the world, the potential for failure is always there. If we put our faith in God, we need not worry. He will never let us down. In the Lord's Prayer, Jesus said, "Thy will be done." We can follow that example.

"Come to me, all you that labour and are heavy laden, and I will give you rest. Take my yoke upon you and learn of me, for I am meek and lowly in heart: and ye shall find rest unto your souls" (Matthew 11:28–29).

The roses in my garden bloom fairest in the spring. Vibrant shades of red and coral and soft shades of pink and yellow greet my eyes, and I breathe in the heady fragrance. As the first explosion tempers with the heat of summer, the petals wilt and then turn brown. If I want new blooms I need to cut into the crisp green stalks angled above a five leaf cluster. Dead-heading the faded flowers is critical to new growth. If I prune, new buds will grow and the roses can bloom till fall. So it is with us.

If we ever want to reach our glorious potential, we must pass through trials with trust in Heavenly Father. Cast aside our fears and self-imposed limitations. Let go of doubts or anger that blind us from truth and find the sweet peace of accepting His will so we can be stronger. Facing adversity once is not enough, it is a process we must repeat and refine. We all have the ability to become like Him, but it only can be if we rid ourselves of whatever is in the way.

I know not by what methods rare,
But this I know, God answers prayer.
I know that He has given His Word,
Which tells me prayer is always heard,
And will be answered, soon or late.
And so I pray and calmly wait.
I know not if the message sought
Will come in just the way I thought;
But leave my prayers with Him alone,
Whose will is wiser than my own,
Assured that He will grant my quest,
Or send some answer far more blessed.
—author unknown

NOTES

1 "Each a Better Person," *Ensign*, November 2002, 100.

2 Excerpt from "Stone or Bread," by Francine Bennion, *Ensign*, January 1976.

3 Dallin H. Oaks, "The Atonement And Faith," *Ensign*, April 2010.

4 Adapted from Don Roundy, "I Needed Him That Very Hour" *Ensign*, April 2000.

Chapter 11

Little Things Matter

"The very hairs of your head are all numbered." —Matthew 10:30

She seemed interested in coming to church, and a bit leery. What would it be like? Would her baby cooperate, or would she have to take him out in the hall with his wiggles and fussing? She wanted to believe there was a God. She'd been brought up without religion in her life, but becoming older and a mother gave her a renewed desire to find out if there was a higher power that cared about her.

We discussed going to church the following Sunday. She said she didn't have a skirt or a dress to wear.

"That's okay," I assured her. "We can go shopping, and I will help you find one."

She was doubtful. "I have a hard time finding anything that looks good on me or that I feel comfortable wearing. But if I can find something, I'll go."

My heart soared. I wanted her to learn what I knew. Heavenly Father was real. He loved her and was ready and waiting to bless her life when she turned to him.

After her baby woke up from his morning nap, we got in the car to go shopping. I was sure finding her a dress to wear would be easy. Mindful of her budget, we started at a thrift store. The selection was large and the quality good, I thought certainly she would find something there.

I walked the aisles with her, playing with the baby and pointing out clothing I thought would look good on her. She tried on a few, but nothing seemed right. I could tell her interest was waning; she had other things she wanted to get done that day. We left the store empty-handed.

What should I do? I felt the chance to share an important piece of myself slipping away. I didn't want to push her or insist we spend the rest of the day shopping until we found something that would work. Yet I cared about her so much, and I wanted the Spirit to touch her heart at church; I wanted her to feel different.

Before we headed for home, I suggested one more store. It frequently had good sales and was one I enjoyed going too. I parked the car and she agreed to go inside and take a look. I waited while she got the baby out of his car seat said a short prayer in my heart, asking that she would find the right skirt or dress inside.

We headed straight to the misses section and began to look. Within minutes she stopped at a display of skirts and blouses. "This one is pretty cute," she said, taking it off the rack to show me.

I agreed.

"I wonder if they have one in my size." She thumbed through several skirts. Near the back she found one.

I waited in the sitting area while she went in the dressing room. A few minutes later she came out with it on. It fit perfectly and was on sale. A happy smile filled her face. She bought it and we left.

On the way to the car, the baby started fussing. She fished a cracker out of the diaper bag, handed it to him, and then turned to me.

"I can't believe we walked in and I found a skirt so quickly. It's my favorite color and everything. That's never happened before."

I stopped walking. "I want to tell you something." I hesitated briefly, hoping she would take what I was going to share, the right way. "I said a prayer before we went in the store that you would find something you liked."

Her eyes widened. She stared at me but didn't speak.

I touched her gently on the arm and softened my voice. "I've learned nothing is too little to pray about. Our Father in Heaven loves us, and if it matters to us, it matters to Him." I smiled with conviction.

She still seemed at a loss for words. We made it to the car and got in. The interior was quiet while we drove. In front of her apartment, I got out to help her gather her things. We walked to her door. Once she was settled inside, I gave her a hug. "See you on Sunday?"

She nodded with a sparkle in her eyes. "See you on Sunday."

At least half of all my prayers are about little things and those prayers are the ones that are answered the quickest, sometimes within seconds. Every time that occurs, I am immediately humbled. Heavenly Father is extremely aware of each of us.

Haven't we all had moments where we've wondered how, as one individual among the countless other people on the earth, we can matter to Him? Does He really know who we are and what we need?

I love the scripture in Matthew that answers this question: "Are not two sparrows sold for a farthing? and one of them shall not fall on the ground without your Father [knowing]. But the very hairs of your head are all numbered.

"Fear ye not therefore, ye are of more value than many sparrows" (Matthew 10:29–31).

A young resident physician at Boston Children's Hospital worked long hours traveling between the hospital and his home by bicycle since his wife and young family needed their car. One night he rode home after a long shift, tired, hungry, and discouraged. He needed to give his wife and four small children his time and energy when he got home and also a cheerful attitude, but he was finding it hard to just keep pedaling.

On the way he passed a place that sold fried chicken. He knew he would be a lot less hungry and tired if he could stop and have a piece of chicken on his way home. They were running a sale on thighs or drumsticks for twenty-nine cents each. He checked his wallet and found one nickel.

He stared to pray. He told the Lord his situation and asked if in His mercy, He could let him find a quarter on the side of the road.

He began watching the ground more intently but saw nothing. Trying to have a faith-filled but submissive attitude as he rode, he got closer to the store. Almost exactly across the street he saw a quarter on the ground. With gratitude and relief, he picked it up and bought the chicken. He savored every morsel and rode happily home.[1]

"Therefore ye must always pray unto the Father in my name; And whatsoever ye shall ask the Father in my name, which is right, believing that ye shall receive, behold it shall be given unto you" (3 Nephi 18:19–20).

A former stake president shared this story:

> I was mowing the lawn and needed to plough through the task quickly due to a full Saturday schedule in preparation for stake conference.
>
> When my lawnmower stalled midway through the task, I flipped it on its side and examined the blades, carefully removing the wet grass clippings. I yanked the mow rope to no avail.
>
> I checked and rechecked the gas tank. Plenty of gas. The spark plug looked good. Exasperated, I dropped to my knees to pray. At the conclusion of my simple prayer, I opened my eyes and noticed something I'd missed: a single blade of grass interrupting the flow of current to the spark plug.

Clara McMaster expressed it well in the words of this song:

He gave me my eyes that I might see the color of butterfly wings.
He gave me my ears that I might hear the magical sound of things.
He gave me my life, my mind, my heart I thank him reverently,
for all his creations in which I'm a part.
Yes, I know Heavenly Father loves me.[2]

NOTES

1 Adapted from J. Devn Cornish, "The Privilege of Prayer," *Ensign*, November 2011.

2 Clara W. McMaster, "My Heavenly Father Loves Me," *Children's Songbook* #228.

Chapter 12

When All We Can Do . . . Is Pray

"Trust in the Lord with all thine heart; and lean not unto thine own understanding." —Proverbs 3:5

I watched the minutes tick past and closed my eyes again to try to sleep. Within moments I opened them again, staring at the darkness of my room. My body was tired but my mind refused to relax. Why wasn't my husband home?

The latest his evening appointments at the office had gone before was 10:30 p.m. It was well passed 1:00 a.m. The roads were icy and I worried about his car; it was an older model with rear-wheel drive. I'd tried his cell phone several times and left two voicemails—nothing.

My mind started running on "what-if." What if he had gotten in a car accident on the way home and it was fatal? What if some lunatic had broken into his office building and he'd been shot? What if he was secretly seeing someone else and was with her right now—stop it! I was definitely getting carried away. I rolled over and readjusted my pillow. Out came a sigh. Surely my husband was fine and would have a perfectly reasonable excuse when he came home as to why he was so late. I dozed.

I woke up again and glanced at the clock, it was now 2:30. My husband's side of the bed was still empty. I got up to check for his car. Just in case he had come home and I hadn't heard him. I opened the door off the laundry room and peered into the dark garage, feeling the cooler air nip at my bare feet. I turned on the light—my car was the only one inside. I shivered, relocked the door, and went back to my room.

"Dear Heavenly Father," I prayed. "I'm worried about my husband; he hasn't come home yet from work. Please help him to be safe and come home soon or call me . . ."

I finished my prayer and got back in bed. Another fifteen minutes had passed. Where was he? I was so tired.

A calm feeling entered my heart along with the thought that he'd fallen asleep. I imagined him in his office, typing up the memorandum of understanding after his clients had left—and closing his eyes for a minute. I let out a breath, totally picturing it. He had been putting in long hours lately and that would explain why he hadn't answered his cell phone. He was fine.

At 5:00 the ringing of my phone jarred me awake. I sleepily checked caller ID—it was my husband. "Hello," I said stifling a yawn.

"Oh, wow," he said, "You're not going to believe this but I just woke up."

"Where are you?"

He chuckled. "I'm still at my office. I fell asleep. What time is it?" He paused, then answered the question himself. He must have checked his watch. "5:02." His voice was loud with disbelief.

"I know, I tried calling you several times. I was pretty worried."

"Oh, sorry—ouch, my neck is stiff."

It sounded like he rubbed it. "I can imagine. Are you coming home now?"

He sighed. "Yes, I just need to shut down my computer and lock up. I'll see you soon okay? I love you."

"Love you too. Drive safely." I put down my phone and closed my eyes, hoping the kids would sleep in.

I remember the day a close friend's husband was suddenly killed and I was states away, and the day a family member was put in jail for a crime he didn't commit. I remember the summer my parents had to evacuate their home due to an out-of-control forest fire, and the couple I read about in the paper whose daughter had been abducted.

The time my daughter took the wrong bus and was lost all alone clear across town, or when my son had an important test in geometry he was worried about passing. The day another son had an important job interview, and a sister in my ward went into labor two months early.

I've prayed, and prayed, and prayed some more, staying mindful the only true peace I can find when I can't fix it myself comes from leaving the situation in God's hands.

Lucy Mack Smith, the mother of the Prophet Joseph Smith, prayed often for her family. Her prayers were a source of strength in their home. On one occasion, she pleaded for help for the Prophet and the protection of the gold plates.

She wrote: "That night I sat up very late. . . . About twelve o'clock Joseph came to me and asked me if I had a chest with a lock and key. . . . And not having one I was greatly alarmed. . . . But Joseph . . . said, 'Never mind, I can do very well . . . without it—be calm—all is right.'"

Shortly after, Joseph and Emma left, taking a horse and wagon. "I spent the night in prayer and supplication to God, for the anxiety of my mind would not permit me to sleep."[1]

Prayer is powerful.

It was a Saturday night and my cell phone rang, I didn't hear it. A short time later my husband told me our twenty-three-year-old son working in Alaska for the summer had called and was headed for the hospital.

Immediately, I called him back.

"Hi, Mom," he said. He sounded okay at first and then I heard him take a sharp breath in.

"What's going on?" worry filled my voice.

"I collapsed at work, and they've called an ambulance. I'm headed to the hospital in Fairbanks."

"Fairbanks?"

"It's the closest one that can handle this type of thing. The med station at Denali isn't set up for more than minor emerg—" Another round of pain stopped his words again. "My stomach . . . Mom, I've never felt such intense pain. The ambulance isn't even here yet, and then it's another two hours to get there." His voice faltered. "I . . . I don't know if I'll make it."

Fear clutched my heart, and I forced it away. "It's going to be okay and there is something you can do—pray."

This silence between us this time was different.

"Mom . . ."

I sensed a slight irritation.

"You know I don't pray. That doesn't work for me."

The rejection of something so dear stabbed me hard, even though his words weren't a complete surprise. "Well, I'm going to pray for you."

"Thanks," he said softly.

At least that's something, I thought. He didn't reject the idea of me doing it. "Everything is going to be okay," I told him sounding certain. "You still have your whole life ahead of you."

His pain was building again. "I have to go . . . "

"Call me as soon as you get to the hospital and you know what's wrong." I quickly added, "I love you."

"I love you too."

The phone clicked, and on cue, the tears came. Immediately I knelt down by my bed and began to pray. After I finished, I called the Salt Lake Temple prayer roll to add his name; I talked to his siblings and asked them to pray for him too.

Close to two and a half hours later, he called. The doctor had seen him and they were prepping him for emergency surgery—he had a blockage in his bowel. We talked for less than a minute. I told him again everything would be fine and to call me when he could. He promised.

I went to look for my husband and told him the update. Together we knelt down and prayed all would be well.

The next text I got, my son told me the surgery was successful, the doctor had removed the tumor, and he'd only lost about a foot of his intestine. He'd been advised if much more time had gone past before they were able to operate, he could have lost up to three feet or possibly his life. He also said the pain had lessened considerably. He was in good spirits, which lifted mine.

I was so grateful to my Heavenly Father. Despite the fact I was over three thousand miles away and physically could do little for my son, I knew the prayers of a concerned mother and family had been heard and answered. My son's recovery could not have gone more smoothly; he was back to work ten days later, virtually pain-free.

There are people in my life I love dearly whose choices have taken them far from God. I've spent days and countless sleepless nights filled with worry and concern, and I've cried until my eyes are bloodshot and swollen. I've met with Church leaders, talked to therapists, gotten priesthood blessings, held family fasts, and continued to show them love, but they haven't changed.

When all we can do is pray we must continue to "walk by faith, not by sight" (2 Corinthians 5:7).

And remember, "all things work together for good to them that love God, to them that are called according to his purpose" (Romans 8:28).

NOTES

1 Lucy Mack Smith, ed. Preston Nibley, *History of Joseph Smith* (1979), 102.2.

Chapter 13

Prayer Changes Things

"The eyes of the Lord are over the righteous, and his ears are open unto their prayers." —1 Peter 3:12

My first book was being released soon and I needed an online presence with a website. At the time I had very little extra money to spend on having one done. A few programs online were free, so I decided to make my own. Having no background in web design, it was much harder than I expected even with following an outlined program.

The biggest challenge was with the page layout, getting the margins right and setting up the background colors and specific designs. I wanted several pages with different content, instead of just a basic home page.

Several nights after my children were in bed I stayed up late working on it. It came together slowly, but it didn't look as professional as I wanted. I changed it repeatedly, adjusting things here and there, but it still didn't look right. I was extremely frustrated.

Finally I made it a matter of prayer. I told Heavenly Father what I needed, what I had done, and what the results had been. I then asked for His help. I felt I had gone as far as I could and the deadline was approaching. I ended my prayer saying I was leaving it in His hands.

Two days later I received an email from a commercial web designer. He designed the website for a marriage counselor who had read my book and advertised it on his site. He wanted to know if I wanted him to do a website for me. I was surprised and at the same time concerned. I went to his online profile and saw several sites he had designed—they were well done. I could only imagine how much he would charge.

I sent him an email in reply, thanking him for his offer, but telling him I was on a very limited budget and doubt I could afford his services. He said he understood but had felt prompted he was supposed to help me. He would accept any amount I could pay.

Tears filled my eyes and the Spirit touched my heart; Heavenly Father answered my prayer. The stress and frustration I'd dealt with for weeks was taken away. I was touched that a stranger was so willing to help. He mentioned someone had given him a hand before and he was glad to help me. I planned I would in turn, "pay it forward" to someone else.

The website he designed for me was better than the one I had imagined in my mind. Prayer had changed it.

"Search diligently, pray always, and be believing, and all things shall work together for your good" (Doctrine and Covenants 90:24).

At 1:30 a.m. a member of the fire department in Alberta, Canada, was jolted awake by the sound of his pager. His help was urgently needed. He hurriedly got dressed and looked out the window. He breathed in sharply; one of the homes in the nearby trailer court was engulfed in flames twenty feet high.

Minutes later the fire chief at the scene told him to get his breathing equipment on; he was backup for the team inside the burning home. Feeling half-awake and somewhat disoriented, he saw the leaping flames of fire and felt frightened. He had fought different kinds of fire before but had been with the department for less than a year and never had to go inside a burning building.

He believed serving others was the same as serving God, and his work put this in to practice, but as he watched the flames shoot higher, intense fear practically paralyzed him.

The order came, "You're going in."

The occupants had already made it out, but the mobile homes close by were at high-risk; the fire had to be contained and extinguished. Scared as he was, he ran toward the inferno, praying.

He prayed for his fellow firefighters working by his side. He prayed for the family watching their home burn. He prayed for his wife and children. He prayed for himself and his partner to safely finish the job they needed to do. They could no longer see their way to the other team; the smoke had grown too thick.

He continued praying, and his mind suddenly filled with Lehi's vision of the tree of life. Calmness replaced his fear. He thought about the iron rod and he knew the way to find the other team was to follow the fire hose.

It took fifteen minutes to get the fire under control, and as the smoke cleared he felt overwhelming gratitude for the Lord's help. It was a life-changing experience. The words of the Book of Mormon took on a deeper meaning, and he learned in a powerful way when we serve others, Heavenly Father watches over us and blesses them through our efforts. [1]

His prayer changed what could have been a different outcome of the fire.

"And they did pray unto the Lord their God continually, insomuch that the Lord did bless them . . . that they did wax strong" (Alma 62:51).

A young man of fourteen wanted to visit his father who was stationed at a military base about thirty-five miles away. He planned to catch the bus, but unfortunately he ended up missing it and decided to hitchhike instead.

The man that gave him a ride took him twenty miles west of the city then dropped him off at a smelter. It started to rain and the sky was growing dark. The air was filled with sulfuric fumes from the smelter and the young man started coughing and wheezing. He started to pray. Breathing became more difficult, and his prayers grew more desperate and earnest.

Suddenly, he heard a voice say, "Run." He didn't want to run and ignored the impression. The voice got more distinct: "Run." He started to jog. The voice came a third time, more urgently, "Run as fast as you can!" He sped up.

At the top of a hill he saw a car making a U-turn. He yelled and waved his arms to get the driver's attention. The sound that came from his throat was more like a croak. He couldn't speak coherently, but the car stopped and the couple seemed to understand. They offered him a ride.

He was completely soaked from the cold rain, his body shaking uncontrollably. He got in and they drove away from the area filled with fumes. The couple told him that they had been sitting in their home when they felt that they should take a drive—in the middle of the storm.

A young man's prayer, and a couple following a prompting, saved his life.

"And it is my will that you shall humble yourselves before me, and obtain this blessing by your diligence and humility and the prayer of faith" (Doctrine and Covenants 104:79).

There was a story of a man in Pampas Argentina driving across green fields one extremely hot afternoon. The temperatures were so high, the heat waves were visible. However, he felt confident in his brand-new car, fresh from the factory. It had a large motor that allowed him to travel in comfort, despite the scorching heat.

Without any warning, the temperature gauge began to climb and the motor started showing signs of strain. Before long, it had reached the danger point and the man pulled off on the side of the road and turned off the engine. He had limited knowledge about cars and was extremely frustrated to think something could stop his big new car, but he hoped he could discover what was wrong.

Not long after he lifted the hood, he realized myriad colorful small butterflies had gathered on top of the radiator, choking the cooling process and stopping the car. It wasn't an eagle or a hawk, or something more easily understood; it was just a couple hundred little butterflies combining collective strength.

One prayer may seem small or insignificant, like a single butterfly, but continual prayers or the combined prayers of many coupled with faith can create a significant difference or great change.

In James 5:16, we read, "The effectual fervent prayer of a righteous man [or woman] availeth much."

PRAYER CHANGES ME
I know not how prayer changes things
That miracles may come to be.
But this I know: Prayer lends me wings,
and by God's grace, prayer changes me!

I know not how a simple task,
Prayer-blessed, shines with divinity,
When in good faith God's help I ask,
But this I know: Prayer changes me.

I am a knocker at the door;
I am a seeker at the gate;
I am an asker, who before
My own dear God has learned to wait.

I know not how prayer changes things;
It is a lovely mystery.
But this I know: Prayer lends me wings,
And day by day, prayer changes me!
—Elizabeth Saxon[2]

NOTES

1 Adapted from Tim Schildknecht's "Fighting Fire With Faith," *Ensign*, January 1996.

2 Elizabeth Saxon, http://content.unity.org/homepageArchive/features/prayerChangesMe.html.

"Wherefore my beloved . . . pray unto the Father with all the energy of heart, that ye may be filled with this love, which he hath bestowed upon all who are true followers of his Son, Jesus Christ; . . . that when he shall appear we shall be like him, for we shall see him as he is, that we may have this hope, that we may be purified even as he is pure. Amen." —Moroni 7:48

About the Author

Diony George is a wife, stay-at-home mom of seven, grandmother of three, motivational speaker, and the author of three books. Through her writing and public speaking, she loves helping others draw closer to God. An avid reader whose favorite genre is romantic suspense, Diony also loves to travel, sew, and bake—especially pies and homemade bread. Born and raised in Alaska, she currently resides in Salt Lake City with her husband and family. Diony can be reached through her personal website at www.dionygeorge.com.

0 26575 11893 3